The Daniel 70 Week Prophecy

Cornerstone of all Prophecy

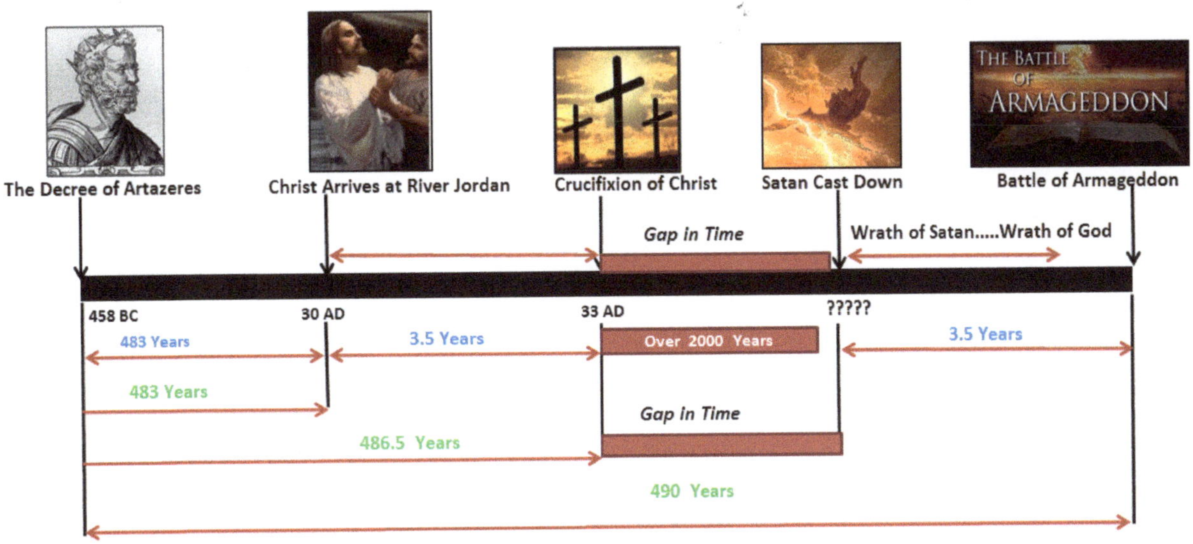

Don T. Phillips

"The Daniel 70 Week Prophecy – Cornerstone of all Prophecy," by Don T. Phillips. 978-1-951985-69-1.

Published 2020 by Virtualbookworm.com Publishing Inc., P.O. Box 9949, College Station, TX 77845, US.

Preface

The Book of Daniel has been a cornerstone of prophecy ever since it was written around 515 BC. Daniel was just a teenager when he was deported from Israel in 606 BC and taken into Babylonian captivity. He was around 90 years old when he wrote the Book of Daniel after nearly 70 years in captivity. In 586 BC Nebuchadnezzar and his army conquered Jerusalem and destroyed the Jewish temple. All but the old and weak were taken into captivity for 70 years for failing to observe the Sabbath day of rest for the land for over 400 years. The Book of Daniel is a remarkable prophetic book. God revealed to Daniel a panoramic world view of future events which would prophesy the rise and fall of 6 great world empires which would begin with the Kingdom of Babylon and end with the completion of the Great Tribulation and the Millennial Kingdom. Hindsight is always more revealing that foresight, and we now know that the visions and prophecies given to Daniel are remarkably an divinely accurate. These visions and prophecies are directed to the Jews and what their ultimate destiny might hold. There have been many fine books written about the Book of Daniel and this one will not just be another verse by verse exposition.

The focus of this book is to examine how Daniel prophecies reveal the 1st and 2nd comings of Jesus Christ and how this current Church Age will end. Although the Book of Daniel was written to the Jews and for the Jews, it has profound implications to all Christians today and the role that Christians will play in the redemption of Israel. In particular, the famous *70 Week Prophecy* of Daniel 9: 1-27 and the final prophecies of Daniel Chapters 10-12 will be the subject of this book.

It will be shown that the prophecies of Daniel 9: 25-27 confirm that Jesus Christ was the long awaited Jewish Messiah who came to redeem all Jews as prophesied by Jeremiah, Joel, Zachariah, Malachi and Zephaniah to name a few. It predicted when the Messiah would arise and that He would be cut off (killed) after a 3.5 year ministry of reconciliation. After Christ had witnessed to the *Jews* for 3.5 years and then crucified on the Cross of Calvary to redeem them from sin, He then turned to the Gentiles after the Feast of Pentecost and the death of Steven to spread the gospel message throughout the known world . The Jews had been temporarily *set aside* and *blinded in part* until the current Church Age would start to come to an end. During this (unknown) period of time in which salvation is offered to Jews and Gentiles alike by faith and grace, the gospel message will be preached to all the world until the *Jewish time of Restoration* will come. The Church Age will not come to an end and Israel restored to a covenant relationship with God until the Great Tribulation described in the Book of Revelation will come to pass. It will be shown that this period of severe tribulation and persecution constitutes the last 3.5 years or the 2nd half of Daniel's 70th week. Again...the book of Daniel is a prophetic panorama of how God will eventually reclaim His chosen people and *all of Israel will be saved;* those who are still alive and accept Jesus Christ as their long awaited redeemer who died for their sins as the Great Tribulation takes place.

In **Chapter 1** the 70 week prophecy of Daniel 9: 27 will be completely discussed and analyzed.

[**24**] *Seventy weeks are determined upon thy people and upon thy holy city, to finish the transgression, and to make an end of sins, and to make reconciliation for iniquity, and to bring in everlasting righteousness, and to seal up the vision and prophecy, and to anoint the most Holy.*
[**25**] *Know therefore and understand, that from the going forth of the commandment to restore and to build Jerusalem unto the Messiah the Prince shall be seven weeks, and threescore and two weeks: the street shall be built again, and the wall, even in troublous times.*
[**26**] *And after threescore and two weeks shall Messiah be cut off, but not for himself: and the people of the prince that shall come shall destroy the city and the sanctuary; and the end thereof shall be with a flood, and unto the end of the war desolations are determined.*
[**27**] And *he shall confirm the covenant with many for one week: and in the midst of the week he shall cause the sacrifice and the oblation to cease, and for the overspreading of abominations he shall make it desolate, even until the consummation, and that determined shall be poured upon the desolate* Daniel 9: 24-27

Two critical questions which must be answered is: (1) Why is it necessary to have a gap in time between the ministry of Christ (His 1st coming as a suffering servant) and His 2nd coming as a conquering King? (2) How does the Daniel 70 week prophecy link to the Great Tribulation as described by John in the Book of Revelation and determine its time?

After an exegesis of Daniel 9: 24-27, There are *four* Critical questions which must be answered in **Chapter 2**: (1) Who issued the decree which initiated Daniel's 70 week prophecy? (2) How was the reign of ancient Kings determined? (3) In which year of the King was the prophecy issued ? and (4) How does this identify the 1st and the last year of Christ ministry ?

It will be shown that the events of the last 3.5 years of Great Tribulation will constitute the *Wrath of Satan* and the *Wrath of God*, and that this will span 1267 days. There are 5 different events will take place over three different periods of time during the last 3.5 years of the tribulation.

Time Period	Start	Finish	Scriptural Reference
42 Months	From When the Beast (Antichrist) Arises	Antichrist is Destroyed at The Battle of Armageddon	Revelation 13:5
42 Months	The Rebuilt Temple will be taken over by Antichrist	The Jewish Temple will be tread Underfoot by Gentiles for 42 Months	Revelation 11:2
1260 Days	Two Witnesses will Start Prophesying	They will prophesy until the Saints (Jews and Gentiles) are Raptured. They will then be killed and lay in street 3.5 days. God will then say: "Come up Here"	Revelation 11:3
1260 Days	Woman is Nourised In wilderness	Until Jesus Comes for Them After Battle of Armageddon	Revelation 12:6
Time, Times and Half a Time	The Woman (Israel) of Revelation 12 is nourished in the wilderness from the dragon (Satan)	The Jews in the wilderness will be nourished to keep them alive so that they can enter the Millennial Kingdom and inherit the Promised land	Revelation 12:14
Time, Times and Half a Time 1267Days	From the Time That the Rebuilt temple in Jerusalem is Descecrated	The Battle of Armageddon	Daniel 12: 1-7
1290 Days 1290 days	by the Antichrist From the Time That the Rebuilt temple in Jerusalem is Descecrated by the Antichrist	The Battle of Armageddon	Daniel 12: 8--11

In **Chapter 3** these 5 events will be placed upon a timeline in the proper place where they occur. The traditional interpretation of all of these events is that they will *each* last 1260 days over a total period of time which is 1260 days, but this is completely illogical. We will show that in general; 3.5 years, 42 months and a time, times and half-a time cannot all be equated to 1260 days. These events do not all start at the same time nor end at the same time. Although this is believed to be a universal assumption which is based upon something called a 30 day *prophetic month* and a 12 month/360 day *prophetic year*, we will try to negate this belief as it applies to Daniel's 70th week prophecy and the Great Tribulation.

The Age of Grace or the Church age has been going on now for almost 2000 years as this book is being penned (30 AD-2020 AD). Many teach and believe that the Church Age will end soon, the saints or the *ecclesia* will be raptured away, and a 7 year period of Great tribulation will begin. It must be understood that regardless of whether the Great Tribulation is 7 years in duration or 3.5 years in duration, severe persecution and tribulation will begin when Satan and his unholy angels are cast out of the heavenlies down to earth by Michael and the Holy angels. At this time and not before will the *Wrath of Satan* fall upon the entire world and then the *Wrath of God* will be unleashed upon all unbelievers. All 5 of the previous events will be placed upon a 3.5 year timeline using 1260 days as the duration of each event. It should be clear that if each of the events and their durations of either 1260 days, 42 months or time, times and half-a time are placed upon a 1260 day timeline that they would start when Satan is cast down and end when Satan is defeated at the *Battle of Armageddon*. This fact does not demands or necessitate a 7 year period of time for the Great Tribulation, but the Wrath of Satan or the Wrath of God cannot begin until Satan is cast down and begins to persecute *all that dwell upon the earth* (Revelation 12:12, Revelation 12:17, Revelation 13:5). At that time, both the Antichrist and the false Prophet will arise (Revelation 13: 1-18). We will clearly show that by any scenario the last 3.5 years of Daniel's 70th week is 1267 days and that the 5 events summarized in the previous table will all fit within this timeframe when their actual duration is determined.

Historical beliefs and false doctrine are not easily overcome, so we will be fair and analyze the last 3.5 years of Daniel's 70th week and the Great Tribulation assuming that these 24 months or time, times and half-a-time are all 1260 days in duration. The duration of the last 3.5 years of tribulation will be assumed to be 1267 days as we will justify. Based upon modern NASA, computer and software development an entirely new analysis of the last 1267 days and the associated 5 events which will occur over that period of time, we will show that 42 months in the Book of Revelation is 1242 days. The 5 events will then be placed upon a timeline which contains other time-related events revealed by both the Old Testament prophets, the Olivet Discourse and the Book of Revelation. This is new and previously unpublished material. Finally, the interaction and prophetic revelation of Daniel 9: 24-27 will be augmented by the end-time-prophecies of Daniel 12: 1-13. In particular, we will offer an interpretation of the 1290 days revealed only in Daniel 12:11 and the 1335 days revealed only in Daniel 12:12.

Chapter 4 Will present scriptural and historical evidence that Christ was crucified in 30 AD.

Chapter 5 will discuss and reveal the Daniel prophecy of end-time events that will occur as the Church Age draws to a close, and will reveal how Daniel predicted the ultimate fate and reconciliation of Israel to the eternal plan of God. Finally, an explanation of the mysterious prophecies of 1290 and 1335 days in Daniel 12: 11-12 will be revealed and discussed as to how they relate to the 1000 year Millennial Kingdom.

Don T. Phillips

September 1, 2020

Dedication

Dedicated to the Gideons Worldwide who labor tirelessly to spread the Gospel Message and win souls to Jesus Christ..... In particular to my friends and fellow Bond-Servants in Jesus Christ or Lord and Savior.

Brother Weldon Mackey
Brother Travis Small
Brother Danny Stribling
Brother Bill Thames

"Now there is in store for me the crown of righteousness,
which the Lord, the righteous Judge, will award to me
on that day—and not only to me, but also to all who
have longed for his appearing." 2 Timothy 4:8

Table of Contents

Chapter 1 Daniel's Prophecy of 70 Weeks 1

Six Things to be Accomplished 4

The Prophetic Timeline 9

Rightly Dividing the Word 10

How Many Days are in 490 Years? 14

The Controversial "He" 18

Grammatical Analysis 21

What is to be Accomplished by The Messiah? 21

Grammatical Analysis 21

Why All of the Confusion ? 26

The Gap Theory 29

Daniel as a Dispensational Prophecy 31

Conclusions 33

Chapter 2 Daniel's Prophecy of 70 Weeks 35

The Commandment to Restore the Temple and Rebuild Jerusalem 35

The Beginning of Regnal Years 38

How Was the Reign of Ancient Kings Determined? 40

The Reign of Artaxerxes I 41

The 7th Year of Artaxerxes Reign 43

The Arrival of Messiah 483 Years After the Decree of Artaxerxes 48

The Birth of Christ and the Daniel Prophecy 48

Chapter 3 A Chronology and Timeline for The Great Tribulation 52

Traditional Interpretation 52

The Reign of Antichrist 54

The Rebuilt Temple Will be Desecrated for 42 Months 56

Two Witnesses Will Prophesy for 1260 Days 57

The Woman is Fed in A Place Prepared by God for 1260 Days 60
The Woman is Nourished in the Wilderness for a Time, Times and Half-a-Time 61
A New Interpretation 63
The Reign of Antichrist 67
The Rebuilt Temple Will be Desecrated for 42 Months 69
Two Witnesses Will Prophesy for 1260 Days 71
The Woman is Fed in A Place Prepared by God for 1260 Days 74
The Woman is Nourished in the Wilderness for a Time, Times and Half-a-Time 76
Exegesis 77
Chapter 4 The Death of Jesus Christ 80
The Crucifixion of Our Lord Jesus Christ 80
The 1st Passover 80
The 2nd Passover 80
The 3rd Passover 80
The 4th Passover 81
Nisan 14, 30 AD is the Correct Date and Year 82
The Seven Feasts of Israel and the Seven High Sabbath Days 84
How Long Did Jesus Christ Lay in the Grave 86
A Wednesday, Nisan 14 Crucifixion 93
A Friday, Nisan 14 Crucifixion 94
A Thursday Crucifixion 98
Summary and Conclusions 99
Daniels 70th Week and Christ Ministry 102
Chapter 5 Daniel and Jewish Destiny 106
Bibliography 114

Chapter 1

Daniel's 70 Week Prophecy

Daniel's Prophecy of 70 Weeks

Daniel is one of the most remarkable persons in the entire Bible. He was never rebuked or criticized for departing from the word of the Lord. He was deported from Jerusalem by Nebuchadnezzar in the first group of exiles in 605 BC, along with Shadrach, Meshach and Abednego. God gave him the gift of interpreting visions and dreams, and he became the 3rd most powerful man in Babylon (Daniel 5:29). After the Persians conquered Babylon in 538 BC under Darius I Daniel continued to serve in the King's palace. In the first year of Darius, he *understood by Books* that the Jewish Babylonian exile would last for 70 years (Daniel 9:2). The *books* were the writings of the prophet *Jerimiah*. Jeremiah began prophesying at age 20 during the 13th year of the reign of King Josiah In the Northern Kingdom of Israel. At the age of 43 he predicted that the southern kingdom of Judah would come to an end, and that Israel would serve the King of Babylon for 70 years (Isaiah 25:11). As Daniel studied the Books of Jeremiah, he realized that 70 years had almost passed. Daniel began a remarkable prayer (Dan 9:1-18) in which he petitioned the Lord to end the captivity as promised, and *turn* (his*) fury from the Holy City of Jerusalem* (Danial 9:16). His prayer was answered by the archangel Gabriel (Dan 9:20). Gabriel is one of only four powerful angels that are named in the Holy Scriptures: *Gabriel, Lucifer, Micheal and Abbadon*.

Gabriel is the only *archangel* named in the KJV, and he is one of three very powerful angels that were created by God to do His bidding: Micheal, Gabriel and Lucifer. Micheal is referred to as the *chief prince* of all good angels. At one time, Lucifer was the most powerful of all angels, but when he rebelled against God he and 1/3 of all the angels previously created by God were cast out of heaven (Revelation 12:4). Micheal's special assignment by God is to protect and watch over Israel (Daniel 12:1). When Daniel prayed and fasted to understand the eventual fate of the Jews, the angel Gabriel was sent (Daniel 9:21) to give him *skill and understanding* (Daniel 9:22). A short time later, another angel would come to Daniel to speak of end-time events. This angel was detained for 21 days by the forces of Satan, and he could not break through until Micheal came to help him (Daniel 10: 12-13). Micheal will play an important role as the last 3.5 years of the Great Tribulation begins. He will engage in a heavenly conflict with Satan and his angels to protect the Jewish people from death and destruction.

Throughout the history of the world, God has caused events to occur which would be so dramatic and significant that they woud change the history of the world. Gabriel is generally regarded as God's messanger to speak great truths to His people. It was Gabriel who was sent to Zachariah to announce that by a virgin birth his wife Mary would be the mother of Jesus Christ. About 6 Months earlier, Gabriel came to Elizabeth to bring her her the news that she would have a son named John . Daniel had previously seen Gabriel in a vision and in Daniel 9 he now comes to speak to him personallyThe prayer which Daniel offered up to God should be taught in every church. It is a model of a sincere, effective prayer. The information given to Daniel by God through Gabriel should be carefully noted.

[15] *And now, O Lord our God, that hast brought thy people forth out of the land of Egypt with a mighty hand, and hast gotten thee renown, as at this day; we have sinned, we have done wickedly.*
[16] *O Lord, according to all thy righteousness, I beseech thee, let thine anger and thy fury be turned away from thy city Jerusalem, thy holy mountain: because for our sins, and for the iniquities of our fathers, Jerusalem and thy people are become a reproach to all that are about us.*
[17] *Now therefore, O our God, hear the prayer of thy servant, and his supplications, and cause thy face to shine upon thy sanctuary that is desolate, for the Lord's sake.*
[18] *O my God, incline thine ear, and hear; open thine eyes, and behold our desolations, and the city which is called by thy name: for we do not present our supplications before thee for our righteousness, but for thy great mercies.*
[19] *O Lord, hear; O Lord, forgive; O Lord, hearken and do; defer not, for thine own sake, O my God: for thy city and thy people are called by thy name* Daniel 9: 15-19

Daniel first praises the Lord God Almighty for what He has already done for His people. This is no small thing; Daniel and the Jews have been in Babylonian captivity for almost 70 years. A person of lesser faith might assume that God has abandoned His people, and even been angry. Daniel knows that his people had been proud and rebellious, and he freely admits it. He is prefacing his request with an understanding that the people deserve nothing but what they got but he appeals to God's love and mercy. He begs God to turn His anger and fury away because He is *righteous*. He pleads that God would restore His people to a place of favor and to restore the Holy Temple and the City of Jerusalem which is lying desolate. This is possibly a play on words. Daniel is specifically praying that the house of God would be restored but he is also aware that this earthly tabernacle of flesh and blood has become inherently evil, and he asked God to restore the righteousness of His chosen people. However, he is quick to ask that God should relent.. not through the righteousness of His people.... but because He is merciful. No one can fully come to Jesus Christ until they realize that *all have sinned and fallen short of the glory of God*. Any righteousness which is in anyone is imputed to that person by Jesus Christ who said: *None are righteous...no not one*. As Daniel was praying, he the angel Gabriel suddenly appeared to Him in person. This was not a dream or a vision...it was a personal visit from Gabriel who had no doubt been sent by God. Gabriel *talked* with Daniel.

[20] *And whiles I was speaking, and praying, and confessing my sin and the sin of my people Israel, and presenting my supplication before the LORD my God for the holy mountain of my God;*
[21] *Yea, whiles I was speaking in prayer, even the man Gabriel, whom I had seen in the vision at the beginning, being caused to fly swiftly, touched me about the time of the evening oblation.*
[22] *And he informed me, and talked with me, and said, O Daniel, I am now come forth to give thee skill and understanding.*
[23] *At the beginning of thy supplications the commandment came forth, and I am come to shew thee; for thou art greatly beloved: therefore understand the matter, and consider the vision* Daniel 9: 20-23

Daniel was confessing both the *sins of the people* and *his own sins*. He is praying not only for his own house and family, but for the house of God in Jerusalem and for the Holy City itself. What humility and humbleness. The response of God should be a blessing and comfort to every Christian. Even while Daniel is praying, God sent Gabriel to answer his prayers. God knew what Daniel wanted to know and understand before he even finished his prayer. The angel spoke to Daniel and told him something amazing: *I am now come forth to give thee skill and understanding.* This should be the answer to almost every prayer that is offered up to God. Many times we simply praise God for who He is and for what He has done...just as Daniel did...but many times we fail to pray for divine wisdom and understanding. In this church age we should realize that every Christian has been given the gift of the Holy Spirit who will give us wisdom and understanding if we will just ask. Most Christians never use the power, wisdom and understanding that the Holy Spirit brings to every Christian. Gabriel had been sent to Daniel even as he began to pray. Even today God will hear our prayers and answer. Gabriel then spoke the words that every Christian longs to hear from his or her Lord and Savior.

for thou art greatly beloved: therefore understand the matter, and consider the vision
Daniel 9:23

Daniel was *greatly loved* by God. He refused to bow down to the idols and graven images of Nebuchadnezzar.....He refused to eat food that was Jewish unclean....He refused to call anyone god except Jehovah God..... and he evidently treated everyone with love and respect, even if he disagreed with them. Each of us should have that attitude and commitment as we journey through life. Daniel's prayer had been answered and the Lord then revealed to Daniel what would happen to his people. The restoration of Israel will not come to pass until the Jews recognize and accept His Son as their long awaited Messiah. The answer to Daniel's is the prayer and the fate of Israel is the mysterious and important 70 week prophecy of Daniel.

[24] *Seventy weeks are determined upon thy people and upon thy holy city, to finish the transgression, and to make an end of sins, and to make reconciliation for iniquity, and to bring in everlasting righteousness, and to seal up the vision and prophecy, and to anoint the most Holy.*
[25] *Know therefore and understand, that from the going forth of the commandment to restore and to build Jerusalem unto the Messiah the Prince shall be seven weeks, and threescore and two weeks: the street shall be built again, and the wall, even in troublous times.*
[26] *And after threescore and two weeks shall Messiah be cut off, but not for himself: and the people of the prince that shall come shall destroy the city and the sanctuary; and the end thereof shall be with a flood, and unto the end of the war desolations are determined.*
[27] *And he shall confirm the covenant with many for one week: and in the midst of the week he shall cause the sacrifice and the oblation to cease, and for the overspreading of abominations upon the desolate* Daniel 9: 24-27

This prophecy is considered to be the most important in the entire Holy Bible. It spans a period of time from when a commandment went forth from the King to Ezra the scribe to rebuild the temple and the city to the second coming of Jesus Christ. Hence, this prophecy begins with the *going forth of the commandment to restore and to build (rebuild) Jerusalem.* It also predicts when the Messiah would arise and when He would be crucified. It will be shown in Chapter 2 that the decree which initiated the 70 week prophecy of Daniel was issued by the Persian King Artaxerxes in 458 BC, in the 1st year of his reign in the Jewish month of Tishri. Daniel 9: 24-27 is filled with mystery and ambiguity. It was given to Daniel and it concerned only Israel. The revelation is directed to (1) *thy people....* The nation of Israel and (2) *thy holy city....* Jerusalem.

Six Things to be Accomplished

Seventy weeks are determined upon thy people and upon thy holy city, to finish the transgression, and to make an end of sins, and to make reconciliation for iniquity, and to bring in everlasting righteousness, and to seal up the vision and prophecy, and to anoint the most Holy Daniel 9:24

The time given to accomplish all aspects of this prophecy is given in Daniel 9:24 as *70 weeks.* The Hebrew word translated as "weeks" is *shabua* It means 7 periods of time....days, weeks, years....etc. to be determined in context. This phrase has been studied in great detail for hundreds of years and it is universally interpreted as *70 weeks of years.* This means that (70*7)=490 years are allocated for the fulfillment of this prophecy. We will shortly show that the 490 years are not sequential but will be interrupted and delayed for a yet to be determined period of time. There are six things to be accomplished (Daniel 9:24).

(1) finish the transgression
(2) make an end to sins
(3) make reconciliation for iniquity
(4) bring in everlasting righteousness
(5) seal up the vision and prophecy
(6) anoint the most Holy

The six things to be accomplished are arranged in two groups of three. The first three are dealing with the *issue of sin*, and the second three with the *fulfillment of righteousness.* Note again that these six things are to be accomplished by *thy people*...Jews and not the church. We will examine these verses in some detail; they form the cornerstone for all end-times prophecy.

(1) *finish the transgression*

The word translated transgression has a root meaning *to rebel.* In this context, it refers to the Jews' specific sin of rebellion against God. This rebellion was the root cause of Israel's other sins. Gabriel was relating to Daniel that Israel would not stop its rebellion against God and His holy laws until these 490 years would run their course. Scriptures reveal that Israel will not repent, turn to God and be saved until the second coming of Christ at the end of the final Tribulation period. *At that time, all of Israel will be saved.* This is a corporate decree, and not an individual decree. (Zechariah 12:10-13:1; Romans 11:25-27). It is true that each individual must come to Christ on a personal basis, *but just as the body of Christ is one unit, the believing children* of Israel will constitute one unit of individual believers (Leviticus 26:40-42; Jer. 3:11-18; Hos. 5:15) ....a believing remnant. *At that time* Israel's national sin—rejection of her Messiah—will be brought to an end.

(2) *make an end to sins*

The Hebrew word used here for *sins* is *chatta'ath.* It refers to the permanent end of the acts of sin. It cannot refer to the end of the *problem* of original sin as some maintain, or of how Christ dealt with sin on the cross. The sacrificial death of Christ on the cross of Calvary did not put an end to sins at all; it enabled our sins to be permanently forgiven by the shedding of His precious blood . At the cross He dealt with the sin issue in the context that they are to be *remembered* no more and are *forgiven* by grace. The phrase, *put an end to sins* means exactly what it says; to put an end of sin forever. This will only be accomplished when those Jews who survive the Great Tribulation will finally turn to Jesus Christ as their long-awaited Messiah and be saved by faith. This believing remnant will enter into the Millennial Kingdom alive, and inherit the Land of Promise. Sin and rebellion will ultimately reach its prophesied end as the 1000 year Millennial Kingdom will draw to a close when death and sin will be put away, and Satan is cast into the Lake of Burning Fire.

(3) *make reconciliation for iniquity*

The word Hebrew word *kapher* is translated *reconciliation* in this passage, but in the Authorized King James Bible it is usually translated as *atonement*. Iniquity is simply sins. Atonement in the Old Testament always carries the force of a *covering*. In this context it refers to the Levitical sacrificial system which only provided a temporary atonement or covering for sins. The Levitical sacrificial system could never reconcile Israel to God, only the work of Jesus Christ at the cross could do that. The Apostle Paul revealed that: God *was in Christ , reconciling the world to Himself, not imputing their transgressions unto them; and hath committed unto us the word of reconciliation* (II Corinthians 5:19). *For if when we were enemies, we were reconciled to God by the death of his Son* (Romans 5:10). This is a difficult passage, but it can only mean that a time would come when sins would be forgiven by the work of Christ upon the cross, and that this would permanently forgive sins...not just cover them. The sin issue was settled at the cross, and any further sacrifices of bulls and goats are an insult to Jesus Christ who shed His own blood to permanently forgive sins....past, present and future. When Christ sacrificed Himself as the perfect Lamb of God it ended the Levitical sacrificial system forever: *For it is not possible that the blood of bulls and of goats should take away sins* (Hebrews 10:4). The Roman Catholic ritual of administering last rites to a dying person so that sins can be confessed and forgiven before death is an insult to Jesus Christ. It must be realized that the shed blood of Jesus Christ on the Cross of Calvary was not an atonement for sins, but a permanent and everlasting sacrifice for individual sins. How many times must our Lord Jesus Christ pay the price for sins? ...only once.

(4) *bring in everlasting righteousness*

It is written that *There is none righteous, no, not one* (Romans 3:10). The only righteous person that ever existed on Earth is Jesus Christ our Lord. Any righteousness attributed to man is *imputed* by Christ. The argument concerning the phrase *bring in everlasting righteousness* is usually that righteousness was ushered in forever when Christ died on the cross. There is no denying that through his sacrificial death that we can now claim some measure of righteousness by accepting Christ as our savior, but we are not fully righteous until victory over this life is claimed at death, and we stand *without spot or wrinkle*, blameless before the throne of God. Sin and unrighteousness will continue to exist until we are fully transformed into the righteousness of Christ. The apostle John saw this fulfilled when he penned the Book of Revelation.

And I heard as it were the voice of a great multitude, and as the voice of many waters, and as the voice of mighty thundering, saying, Alleluia: for the Lord God omnipotent reigns. Let us be glad and rejoice, and give honor to Him: for the marriage of the Lamb is come, and his wife hath made herself ready. And to her it was granted that she should be arrayed in fine linen, clean and white: for the fine linen is the righteousness of saints Revelation 19: 6-8.

(5) *seal up the vision and prophecy*

The subject of Biblical prophecy is a lifelong journey. Prophecy probably takes up more verses in the Holy Scriptures than any other subject. The entire Book of Revelation is prophecy between Revelation Chapter 6 and Chapter 23. Contrary to what some may teach, prophecy and prophets exist in the church today and will continue to exist until the end of the church age. There are those who teach that the gift of healing was an apostolic gift are just wrong: Paul said:

And God hath set some in the church, first apostles, secondarily prophets, thirdly teachers, after that miracles, then gifts of healings, helps, governments, diversities of tongues I Corinthians 12:26

When one reads the directive to *seal up the vision and prophecy.....* The vision is the collective content of the entire prophecy given to Daniel. Vision and prophecy will be sealed up or finished when Christ returns a 2nd time and establishes His 1000 year kingdom here upon this earth. If one reads this verse without bias or preconceived notions, then the issue of a *gap* between the death of Christ and his second coming should be uncontested. The only question to be answered is , how long is this *gap* or *period of time*? Christ himself answered this question when he gave the Olivet Discourse shortly before his crucifixion.

But of that day and hour knoweth no man, no, not the angels of heaven, but my Father only Matthew 24:36

At the end of the Age of Grace when Christ appears, vision and prophecy will be sealed up forever. No one knows when this will occur. The issue of when the Daniel prophecy gap in time begins and ends will be fully addressed later in this Chapter.

(6) *anoint the most Holy*

This is a difficult passage. The word translated *anoint* is from the Hebrew word *mashiyach*, which means to *set aside or consecrate for a holy purpose***.** There have been two primary interpretations. The first interpretation is that the *most holy* refers to our *Lord Jesus Christ*. This interpretation has little merit, since Jesus Christ needs no anointing. He was and is the only Son of God, and He was anointed by the Father.

How God anointed Jesus of Nazareth with the holy ghost and with power: who went about doing good, and healing all that were oppressed of the devil; for God was with Him
Acts 10:38

The second interpretation is that the *most Holy* is the *Millennial Temple*. Any Jew would immediately recognize that in the Old Testament, the *most Holy* would be clearly understood to be the *Holy of Holies* in both the tabernacle and the temple, where God came to visit with the High Priest once a year on the Feast of Atonement. Man was separated from God (literally and symbolically) by a curtain that separated the Holy Place from the Holy of Holies. It was enormous, 45 to 60-foot high and four inch thick. This curtain spiritually separated man from God, and it was rent from top to bottom when Christ cried out *it is finished* as he died on the cross of Calvary. The temple and the Holy of Holies were completely destroyed in 70 AD by the Roman army. It will be rebuilt just north of Jerusalem in Shiloh when the Millennial Kingdom begins. The new temple is described in (Phillips, *The Millennial Kingdom*) . It will be the center of worship in the 1000 year Millennial Kingdom.

And it shall come to pass, that everyone that is left of all of the nations which came against Jerusalem (at the Battle of Armageddon) shall even go up from year to year to worship the King, the Lord of hosts, and to keep the Feast of Tabernacles Zechariah 14:16.

The phrase *most Holy* is taken from the Hebrew words *qodesh qoddashem*, which means *the Holy of Holies*. It is therefore concluded that this part of the prophecy refers to the cleansing, anointing and dedication of the cleansed temple in the Millennial Kingdom.

It is important to realize once again that that this prophecy concerns the Jews and only the Jews. Jesus Christ was born, lived and died as a Jew. Simply reexamine each of these 6 parts of this prophecy and ask..... *Who will accomplished each one?* The answer is Jesus Christ the Son of God. Another way to reach this same conclusion is to ask: Did Satan or the Antichrist *finish the transgression*? No. Did Satan or the Antichrist *make an end to sins*? This is a ridiculous question. Did Satan or the Antichrist *Make reconciliation for iniquity*? Of course not. Did Satan or the antichrist *seal up vision and prophecy*? The Antichrist never sealed up anything. Did Satan or *the Antichrist ever anoint the most Holy* ? Of course not. The focal point of this entire prophecy is Jesus Christ. The term Antichrist never even appeared in the Old Testament, and he was never fully revealed until after the Old Covenant passed away (I John 2: 18 22, I John 4:3, II John 1:7). The *beast that will arise* in Revelation 13:1 has been called *the Antichrist*. That is only a title that has been given to that evil individual The Old Testament Jews also never knew Jesus Christ by name, but the Old Testament is full of prophecies concerning a Jewish Messiah who would redeem them from sin.

The Prophetic Timeline

Daniel 9:25-26 divides the prophetic timeline into 3 separate periods of time. The *commandment to rebuild Jerusalem* would immediately initiate the 490 year prophecy. The 1st period of time is *seven weeks* (49 years), followed by *threescore and two weeks* (62 weeks or 434 years). Gabriel immediately reveals that: *the street shall be built again, and the wall, even in troublous times* (Daniel 9:24b). Evidence in the books of Ezra, Nehemiah and Zachariah indicate that the temple and the walls took about 49 years to complete. The people were constantly under duress by outside forces. After the initial 49 years there would be 434 years which would pass *unto Messiah the Prince*. This period of time included 400 years of silence during which there were no prophets in the land. The *400 Years of Silence* is the name given to the period of time between the last of the Old Testament prophets and the arrival of Jesus in the New Testament. This period of time was between the prophet Malachi and the ministry of John the Baptizer at the River Jordan. After 483 years Jesus Christ would come to the River Jordan to be Baptized into His 3.5 year ministry of reconciliation to the Jews. *And after threescore and two weeks shall Messiah be cut off, but not for himself* (Daniel 9:26). The phrase *cut off* in the Greek means *to be killed*. Christ was crucified on Passover, Nisan 14, which was 3.5 years after the 70th week of Daniel started at the River Jordan. In Chapter 2 we will prove beyond a reasonable doubt that Jesus Christ came the River Jordan in the fall of 26 AD and was crucified in 30 AD. He was perfect in every way and lived a sinless life; He did not need to be beat, tortured and crucified for Himself. His sacrificial death was for the forgiveness of sin....Jews and Gentiles alike. He was the perfect, sinless Lamb of God (John 1:29).

Recall that in Daniel 9:24 there were 6 things to be accomplished in the 490 year prophecy.

to finish the transgression, and to make an end of sins, and to make reconciliation for iniquity, and to bring in everlasting righteousness, and to seal up the vision and prophecy, and to anoint the most Holy *Daniel 9:24*

When Christ was crucified He did not accomplish all of these 6 eternal objectives. He will...but not until the end of the Great tribulation at His 2nd advent. Hence, there must be a gap in the Daniel prophecy. The question is...WHEN? There are really only two choices: (1) When Christ came to the River Jordan after 483 years had elapsed or (2) When He was crucified after 486.5 years.

Rightly Dividing The Word of God

At the risk of redundancy, it must be forcefully stated once again that this prophecy is directed to *thy people*....the Jews ...and not to the church. The choice of when a gap appears in the 480 years can only be found by realizing that God deals with His creation in different ways over different periods of time. These periods of time are called *dispensations (*Phillips, *The Eternal Plan of God*). There are 7 different dispensations of time in God's eternal plan for mankind, but the two most prominently in view here are the *Dispensation of the Law* and the *Dispensation of Grace*. God has had only one plan ever since He created the Adam and Eve in the Garden of Eden. He has desired to walk and talk with man...commune with man...and function in an intimate, personal relationship with man. This desire and plan was interrupted when Adam and Eve sinned. God cannot tolerate sin and so He left the Garden of Eden and banned Adam and Eve from ever walking there again. Adam and Eve had sinned against God, and the Wages of sin is death. There is only one remedy for death...and that is life. To fulfill His original plan for man, God sent His only Son to pay a great price for the permanent forgiveness of sin....past, present and future. These entire 3.5 years Christ is speaking to the Jews. After choosing His 12 disciples He instructed them:

These twelve Jesus sent forth, and commanded them, saying, Go not into the way of the Gentiles, and into any city of the Samaritans enter ye not Matthew 10:5

The ministry of Christ was to the Jews and not to the church. The entire Church Age or Age of Christ was completely unknown to the Jews until God chose Saul of Tarsus (Paul) to reveal it to the Gentiles.

How that by revelation he made known unto me the ***mystery****; (as I wrote afore in few words* Ephesians 3:3

[26] *Even the* ***mystery*** *which hath been hid from ages and from generations, but now is made manifest to his saints:*

[27] *To whom God would make known what is the riches of the glory of this* ***mystery*** *among the Gentiles; which is Christ in you, the hope of glory* Colossians 1: 26-27

Paul and Barnabus first took it to the Jews, and when they were completely rejected they turned to the Gentiles.

Then Paul and Barnabas waxed bold, and said, It was necessary that the word of God should first have been spoken to you: but seeing ye put it from you, and judge yourselves unworthy of everlasting life, lo, we turn to the Gentiles Acts 13: 46

The sacrificial death of Christ and the shedding of His blood on the Cross of Calvary removed the curse of sin. This was the act of *Justification*. Sinful man can now go boldly before

God and He will see them as righteous....not in their own body...but in the body of our Lord Jesus Christ (Romans 6:3, Galatians 3:27). Although the issue of sin was settled by Christ on the Cross, *righteousness* can only be imputed to sinful man by faith...Faith in the atoning work of Jesus Christ, faith that He is the Son of God and faith that just as He conquered death by being raised from the dead we will also. Once a person believes these things and accepts Christ as their Lord and Savior God sends us the gift of the Holy Spirit, and that person is baptized into Christ. That person is then a new creature in Christ.

When Christ arrived at the River Jordan to begin His earthly ministry, man was still under the Law of Moses. Salvation was offered to the Jews and not to the Gentiles. Christ said: *These twelve Jesus sent forth, and commanded them, saying, Go not into the way of the* ***Gentiles****, and into any city of the Samaritans enter ye not* (Matthew 10:5).

Every Christian who is alive today should realize that the entire earthly ministry of Jesus Christ was directed to the Jews. He offered salvation to the Jews through one path... be baptized unto repentance and be saved by their long awaited Jewish redeemer and Messiah....Jesus Christ the Son of God. This might come as a surprise to most Christians today. The Gospels of Matthew, Mark, Luke and John recorded His earthly ministry to the *Jews*. Of course, all of God's Holy word is truth and much of what He said can also apply to the Gentiles, but the plan of salvation to both Jews and Gentiles by faith and grace was completely hidden from the Jews. It was not revealed until God chose the apostle Paul to preach the gospel message of the New Covenant to Jews and Gentiles alike. The entire Church Age was a *mystery* not revealed in times past, but was made manifest by Paul who was specifically chosen to preach the message of Salvation to the Gentiles. Sadly, this is still a mystery to the corporate body of the Jews who refuse the grace and mercy of Jesus Christ. Do not be deceived...the Law of Moses, particularly the 10 commandments, was good and holy because it was given by God. However, salvation could never be attained under the Law. No man could live under the law without breaking the law. The Law was a *taskmaster* to teach the Jews that no one could ever be justified under the law. Justification was promised by all of the Old Testament prophets through a future Messiah who would be sent by God to take away all sins. That Messiah was Jesus Christ. Every Jew can only be saved in one way...by faith and grace. Jesus said: *I am the way, the truth and the life. No man cometh unto the Father but by me.* There will be a believing remnant who will turn to Jesus Christ during this Age of Grace, but corporately the Jews will remain in disbelief until they finally accept Christ as their Messiah during the Great Tribulation....and so *All of Israel will be saved* (Romans 11:26).

Why is it so important to read the bible as a dispensational document? It is the key to understanding the 70 Week Prophecy of Daniel and the purpose of the Great Tribulation. Understanding the eternal plan of God will clearly reveal that the 490 years of Daniel 9: 24-27 must be suspended at some point in time to allow God to reclaim His chosen people, the Jews and to fulfill His Land Covenant with the Jews. This cannot take place until *after* the Church age ends and the Millennial Kingdom begins. God cannot annul the unilateral Land Covenant that He made with Abraham and reinforced to Moses and King David. It is hopefully now made clear that the 490 year Daniel Prophecy must be suspended when God turns away from His beloved Jews and offers salvation ...to Jews and Gentiles alike....through the Gentiles. This cannot happen until Christ has died on the Cross of Calvary. *Has it ever occurred to you that the both the earthly ministry of Christ (to the Jews) was 3.5 years in duration, and that the Great Tribulation which will bring the Jews once again back into a covenant relationship with God also takes place over a 3.5 year period of time?* Oh how far above the mind of man is the mind and plans of God! When the prophecy to Daniel was initiated by a decree to rebuild the *Holy City and the Temple,* God began to deal with Israel over 3 sequential time periods: (1) an initial period of 7 weeks ...49 years, (2) a second period of 62 weeks.... 434 years, and then (3) a period of 3.5 years. This is a continuous period of time which lasted 486.5 years starting with a decree to go forth and ending at the Cross of Calvary. God then set aside (not abandoned) His chosen people the Jews and began the Age of Grace...the Church age...during which the Body of Christ will be formed. The first 3.5 years of the ministry of Christ was to the *Jews. When will God once again resume dealing with the Jews ?* This will start when the last 3.5 years of Daniel's 490 year prophecy begins. These last 3.5 years will when Satan is cast down to the earth and the Wrath of Satan, followed by the Wrath of God. will commence....the *Great Tribulation.*

[**15**] *When ye therefore shall see the abomination of desolation, spoken of by Daniel the prophet, stand in the holy place, (whoso readeth, let him understand:)*

[**21**] *For then shall be great tribulation, such as was not since the beginning of the world to this time, no, nor ever shall be* Matthew 24: 15, 21

Shortly after Satan being cast down to earth (Revelation 12), he will attack Jerusalem, desecrate the new temple and fulfill Matthew 24:15. Then there will be *Great Tribulation.*

Do not be deceived or confused. The previous discourse has been presented to justify that there will be a gap in time of unknown duration in the Daniel 490 year prophecy to the Jews. It cannot take place until Jesus Christ finishes His 3.5 ministry of redemption to the Jews...not the Gentiles. When God begins the Church Age He will turn to the Gentiles to preach the gospel message. This is divine, perfect Logic. almost all prophecy teachers interrupt Daniel's Prophecy at the River Jordan and ignore the 3.5 year ministry of Christ to the Jews or they allow the last 7 years of the Daniel Prophecy to expire when Steven is stoned. Both fail to understand the eternal plan of God. This discontinuation of Daniels 490 year prophecy when Christ begins His ministry to the Jews will leave 7 years for the Great Tribulation: And the 7 seals, the 7 trumpets and the 7 bowls take place in *series* over that 7 last years. However, as the 7 seals are broken they are not sequential with the trumpet and Bowl judgments, but they reveal general conditions and several key events which will take place over the last 3.5 years (See Phillips, The Book of Revelation: *Mysteries Revealed* for a complete development of this conclusion). As the 7 seals are broken, John is shown an overview of things which must take place over the last 3.5 years. There are many clues in the Holy Scriptures that this is true, but only one prophetic event needs to be explained to justify this position. In Revelation 6:11 the 6th seal is broken and the following things happen.

[12] *And I beheld when he had opened the sixth seal, and, lo, there was* ***a great earthquake****;*
and the ***sun became black*** *as sackcloth of hair, and the* ***moon became as blood****;*
[13] *And the* ***stars of heaven fell*** *unto the earth, even as a fig tree casts her untimely figs, when she is shaken of a mighty wind.*
[14] *And the* ***heaven departed as a scroll*** *when it is rolled together; and* ***every mountain and island were moved out of their places*** Revelation 6: 12-14

If this is a prophetic revelation of what must take place later, when will it happen? There is a ***great earthquake*** which will take place as the **7th Trumpet sounds** almost 3.5 years later; the **stars fall from heaven**; and ***every*** **mountain and island were moved out of their places** (Revelation 16: 17-20). The prophet Joel verifies that the events associated with the 6th seal being broken on the Scroll of Truth take place immediately before the Battle of Armageddon.

[13] Put ye in the sickle, for the harvest is ripe: come, get you down; for the press is full, the fats overflow; for their wickedness is great.
[14] *Multitudes, multitudes in the* ***valley of decision****: for the* ***day of the LORD is near*** *in the valley of decision.*
[15] *The* ***sun and the moon shall be darkened****, and the* ***stars shall withdraw their shining****.*
[16] *The LORD also shall roar out of Zion, and utter his voice from Jerusalem; and* ***the heavens and the earth shall shake****: but the LORD will be the hope of his people, and the strength of the children of Israel* Joel 3: 13-16

In Revelation 16:11 we are also told exactly when this takes place.....just before the Battle of Armageddon, which ends the Great Tribulation.

[18] *And there were voices, and thunders, and lightnings; and there was* ***a great earthquake,*** *such as was not since men were upon the earth, so mighty an earthquake, and so great.*
[19] *And the great city was divided into three parts, and the cities of the nations fell: and great Babylon came in remembrance before God, to give unto her the cup of the wine of the fierceness of his wrath.*
[20] ***And every island fled away, and the mountains were not found***
Revelation 16: 18-20

Almost every prophecy teacher will present the 7 Seals, the 7 Trumpets and the 7 Bowls of God's Wrath (Revelation 15:1) as occurring sequentially over a 7 year period of time. Use basic logic and read the scriptures....... Are we to believe that **every Mountain and Island would be moved out of its place** two times...7 years apart???? The inescapable conclusion is: ***They cannot***. When the 6th seal is broken the Apostle John is given a vision of what will happen almost 3.5 years later. For those who might be interested in a more complete discussion of why the seals are not sequential with the trumpets and bowls see Phillips; **The Book of Revelation, *Mysteries Revealed.***

How Many Days are in 490 Years ?

In a natural sense, the obvious meaning is that the 490 years will be years of 365.2422 days or a solar year. However, there have been several attempts to interpret each year as a *prophetic year* of 360 days. This book rejects the concept of a 360 day prophetic year being used in this prophecy. *First*, there is absolutely no hint in the Book of Daniel that his prophecies imply or require a 360 day year. *Second*, Daniel was told by Gabriel that he (Gabriel) had come to give him *wisdom and understanding* of the future and fate of the Jews. Surely Gabriel would have told Daniel to base his 490 year revelatory prophecy upon a 360 day year if that was critical to his (Daniels) understanding. Daniel certainly knew that both the Jewish and the Babylonian calendars were constructed to follow both the seasons and new moon days, but both followed a 360.2422 day solar cycle to also predict the seasons. Both the Hebrews and Babylonians used similar calendar adjustments to keep their calendars synchronized with the Sun, moon and equinoxes . Yes, the Egyptian calendar in use at the Exodus from Egypt in 1490 BC was comprised of 12 months of 30 days. Its primary use was to predict when the Nile River would flood each year so that crops could be planted and cultivated. However, when it was implemented by the Egyptians they quickly realized that the seasons were regulated and observed based upon the sun...which demanded a 365.2422 day year. Note that as originally designed, the 360 day Egyptian year would fall back against a 365.2422 day solar year by about 5.25 days every year, and after only 6 years it would predict the spring Nile flood about a month earlier than it would occur. After about 36 years, it would predict spring rains in the winter! To correct the situation, the Egyptians added 5 days to the end of each year. Even that adjustment caused the Egyptian calendar to fall back against a solar year about one day every 4 years. It has been proposed that this is why the Hebrew calendar was instituted by God at the exodus from Egypt. God told Israel to observe the first of each month and the 7 Feasts of Israel perpetually at *exactly* the same time each year, and He gave Moses a perpetual lunar/solar Hebrew calendar that accurately tracked new moon cycles over an average 365.25 day year. *Why is this so hard to believe*? The current Jewish calendar has been used by the Jews for almost 3500 years. It has survived the Babylonian calendar, the Egyptian calendar and the Roman calendar. The Daniel prophecy is based upon a 365.2425 day year as God designed it when He created the heavens and the earth: *And God said, Let there be lights in the firmament of the heaven to divide the day from the night; and let them be for signs, and for seasons, and for days, and years* (Genesis 1:14).

This is not proof that God gave His people a lunar/Solar calendar after the exodus, but it is almost certain that the same Jewish calendar in use today was in use at the time of Christ. Consider the following historical fact verified by both the Jewish Rabbis and the Jewish historian Josephus . It is recorded that Herod's Temple fell to the Roman empire on Saturday, Av 9 in 70 AD. It was ransacked and burned to the ground as predicted 40 years earlier in the Olivet Discourse of Christ. In Chapter 3 we will use modern and complex digital computer software to predict major events in the Book of Revelation. The Jewish calendar of the 1st century is still in use today, and it will still be in use when the Great Tribulation begins. *What would this software calculate for Av 9 in 70 AD?* The following date is calculated by the *Sheppards Page* Computer software and is confirmed by a popular calendar conversion software package called *Hebcal*.

Gregorian:	**August 2, 70** (ante [1])
Julian:	**August 4, 70**
Jewish:	**Av 9, 3830**
	ט׳ באב ג׳תתל״
SDN:	**1746841.5** [2]
Weekday:	**Saturday**

This is the exact date (Julian Calendar date of August 4) and the exact day of the week (Saturday) that both Jewish records and the Historian Josephus record that the walls were breached and the Temple fell. This is only an example that confirms that Jewish historical dates can be confirmed by modern Calendar Conversion software. A complete study was conducted by Carl D. Franklin in 2002 and published as a book: *The Calendar of Christ and His Apostles*. His extensive study verified the modern Hebrew Calendar has been in existence since antiquity. (truthofgod.org)

The heart of Daniels 70 week prophecy will now be discussed.

[25] *Know therefore and understand, that from the going forth of the commandment to restore and to build Jerusalem unto the Messiah the Prince shall be seven weeks, and threescore and two weeks: the street shall be built again, and the wall, even in troublous times.*
[26] *And after threescore and two weeks shall Messiah be cut off, but not for himself: and the people of the prince that shall come shall destroy the city and the sanctuary; and the end thereof shall be with a flood, and unto the end of the war desolations are determined.*
[27] *And he shall confirm the covenant with many for one week: and in the midst of the week he shall cause the sacrifice and the oblation to cease, and for the overspreading of abominations he shall make it desolate, even until the consummation, and that determined shall be poured upon the desolate* Daniel 9: 25-27

A commandment will be issued that will authorize the rebuilding of the desolated temple in Jerusalem and also the City of Jerusalem which was devastated and destroyed in 586 BC by the Babylonian army under the command of Nebuchadnezzar (Daniel 9:24). This commandment will initiate the 490 year prophecy of Daniel. The prophecy is in 3 parts: (1) Seven weeks or 49 years (2) Threescore and two weeks or 434 years and (3) one week of 7 years. This is a total of (483 yrs + 7 Yrs = 490 years). *What is the significance of these 3 time divisions?*

Gabriel commands Daniel to *know and understand*. This reinforces his purpose for coming in Daniel 9:22. This understanding is to begin *from the going forth of the commandment to restore and to build Jerusalem* from some Persian King. We will subsequently show that this king is Artaxerxes I in 458 BC. From the day that this decree is issued a period of 7 weeks will commence. This first unit of 49 years (seven "sevens") covers the time that it took to *rebuild Jerusalem: the street shall be built again, and the wall, even in troublous times* (Daniel 9:25). The second unit of time is 434 years, and it spans the number of years that would elapse from when the Holy City of Jerusalem was rebuilt, the city walls constructed and the Temple restored until *Messiah the Prince* would come. All prophecy students agree that Messiah the Prince is the long awaited Jewish Messiah who was Jesus Christ. *Unto what*? The point in time that is being referenced is when Jesus Christ came to the River Jordan at *about the age of 30* to begin His earthly ministry of reconciliation and repentance of the Jews. Jesus Christ came to the River Jordan exactly 483 years after the decree went forth from a Persian King. The prophecy says that *after* 483 years the Messiah will be *cut off* (killed). The title *Messiah* is Jewish and must refer to a Jew, not a Gentile. In fact, a Gentile was considered to be a heathen and unclean...scum. The Hebrew word for Messiah is *mashiach* which means *the anointed one*. In Judaism the Messiah is the one who would be sent by God to redeem His chosen people and to rule and reign from the Davidic line. This Messiah would arise and free all Jews from the yoke of foreign bondage, redeem them from their sins and restore them to former glory. This is why Jesus Christ was born of the virgin Mary and was the Son of God, and it is why Jesus was a Jew from the tribe of Judah and was in the line of King David through His paternal father, Joseph. The Jews then and now were blinded and simply could not accept Him as their long awaited redeemer. How sad...He satisfied all Jewish expectations and fulfilled all Old Testament prophecies....Every one.

after threescore and two weeks shall Messiah be cut off, but not for himself. The Aramaic term *be cut off* simply means "to be killed".....but not for Himself. Hindsight is always better than foresight, and it is now obvious that this promised Jewish Messiah was crucified 3.5 years after He came to the River Jordan. It should be fully realized that Jesus Christ was born by Mary of God and through that Holy seed He did not inherit the sin of Adam......He was born sinless and lived a perfect, sinless life. Since sin is what separates and alienates man from God, Jesus did not need to ever die....much less die a horrible, torturous death. He could have simply said: *Father I am coming home.* Clearly understand that Christ died a voluntary, hideous death upon the cross to pay the price for all sins...past, present and future. He was crucified to save man from sins, because the *wages of sin is death* (Romans 6:23).....and He did it to glorify the Father (John 17:1). He was the perfect, sinless sacrifice for all sins (I Peter 1:18-19)....When He died on the cross of Calvary he said: *It is finished* (John 19:30).

But God commended his love toward us, in that, while we were yet sinners, Christ died for us
Romans 5:8

Day after day...week after week ....year after year...... the Levitical priesthood sacrificed bulls and goats for the sins of the people. These sacrifices were only an *atonement* for sin: The Greek word translated as *atonement* is *kaphar* and it means to *cover over.* All Old Testament sacrifices for sin only temporarily appeased God until His Son came and permanently forgave all sins. When Christ died as the perfect sacrificial Lamb of God, it was God in the flesh sacrificing Himself for the sins of mankind. We are reminded that when God made a covenant with Abraham He walked between the bloody carcasses of slain animals and established an everlasting, unconditional covenant of blessings with Abraham and his seed. He might turn away for periods of time and allow His chosen people to be persecuted, but He would never break His covenant with Israel. During this current Church Age, the Jews still corporately refuse to believe that Jesus Christ is their promised Messiah. They will remain blinded (in part) until the church age ends at the Battle of Armageddon. It is generally not recognized by Western Hemisphere Christians but the purpose of the Great Tribulation is to restore the Jews through Christ to a covenant relationship with God. As the Tribulation period comes to an end, *all of Israel* (Romans 11:26).....those who are alive and remain.... will come to Christ and inherit the

Kingdom promised to Abraham, Moses and King David (Phillips, *The Millennial Kingdom*). We can now understand why Christ was *cut off*...but *not for Himself.* Daniel 9:26 can also be understood looking back in time.

the people of the prince that shall come shall destroy the city and the sanctuary; and the end thereof shall be with a flood Daniel 9: 26

The angel Gabriel now looks far into the future and predicts the destruction of Herod's Temple and the City of Jerusalem by Titus and his Roman army in 70 AD. God had given the Jews 40 years to turn to His Son Jesus Christ and be saved...but they would not. After 40 years (30 AD - 70 AD) God allowed the Holy City and His Holy Temple to be destroyed by evil, ruthless people. They were the Roman Centurions who were doing the work of Satan. The end came quickly after the temple walls were breached on Av 9, 70 AD. The Roman soldiers passed through the city and the temple in a *flood of destruction*. From this point on, the Jews experienced tribulation and suffering *because they refused to accept Jesus Christ as their Savior. The dark ages....Hitler's 3rd* Reich...the temple site which now belongs to the Muslims and the occupation of Israel's land by Palestine today.... were all relentless persecution of the Jews. The persecution and anti-Semitism has gone on almost 2000 years now and will not cease until wars will end at the 2nd coming of Christ.

We will show in Chapter 2 that Christ died in 30 AD. When Christ died the veil of the temple was *rent in two*. The veil separated the Holy of Holies from the Holy Place, where God came to commune with the high priest once a year on the Feast of Atonement. No one could go any farther than the Holy Place but the High Priest. When Christ died He became both our advocate and our Great High Priest forever. Man can now boldly come before the throne of God and stand in His presence because God no longer sees us as full of sins but justified and forgiven of all sin by the blood of His Son. We are baptized into Christ by the Holy Spirit (I Corinthians 12:13). When God sees a born-again Christian He no longer sees a common sinner but He sees the righteousness of Christ. It is beyond comprehension what God in Christ has done for every sinner. He offers us salvation and eternal life by *faith* and *Grace*. Christ did for man that which no man could never do for Himself. Praise God and His Son forever! There is a prince who will seek to deceive and destroy sinful man. He is called Lucifer or Satan. Satan is now the *Prince of Power of the Air* (Ephesians 2:2). He will arise as the Antichrist in the Great Tribulation and will deceive many. Salvation is an individual act of faith. Choose life...or choose death. The choice is up to you.

The Controversial "*He*"

We now come to one of the most controversial and difficult passages in the entire Bible.

*And **he** shall confirm the covenant with many for one week: and in the midst of the week **he** shall cause the sacrifice and the oblation to cease, and for the overspreading of abominations* **he** *shall make it desolate, even until the consummation, and that determined shall be poured upon the desolate* Daniel 9:27

The difficulty in interpreting exactly what Daniel 9:27 means is to identify the antecedent of the personal pronoun, ***he***. There are two primary schools of thought: The 1st is that the personal pronoun he refers to the Messiah...Jesus Christ, and the 2nd is that it refers to the Antichrist. To discover truth, it is necessary to understand the purpose of Daniel's 70 week prophecy in the first place. Gabriel came to Daniel to give him *wisdom and understanding*. There is every indication that Daniel understood this prophecy and its main implications. A Messiah appearing in the far future to redeem the House of Israel was known by all Jews and was prophesied throughout the books of the new testament. Daniel or anyone else could not identify Jesus Christ as that promised Messiah, but it was certain that one would be sent by God to fulfill His eternal purposes. The Church Age and salvation by grace was not known to the Old Testament prophets, Jews or Gentiles until God anointed, appointed and chose the Apostle Paul to reveal this truth after the crucifixion of Christ on the Road to Damascus (Ephesians 3: 2-5). The great tribulation period of time which would terminate the current church age was spoken of by Denial in his amazing visions, and Christ added more details during His famous Olivet Discourse just before He was crucified. Although sometimes obscured and clothed in mystery the person that was to be known as the Antichrist was mentioned by Ezekiel, Joel, Jeremiah, Zachariah and other prophets of God in their prophetic writings. The full meaning and import of these truths was not fully revealed until God called the Apostle John to pen the apocalyptic Book of Revelation.

It is proposed here that the personal pronoun *he* must refer to the promised Jewish Messiah who is Jesus Christ. This conclusion is supported by the following line of thought. The 70 week prophecy is entirely directed to the redemption of the Jewish people. This redemption was offered to the Jewish people by Jesus Christ during His 3.5 years of ministry. Christ was born, lived and died a Jew. It must be understood that the entire 3.5 ministry of Jesus Christ was conducted under the Old Covenant. He lived under the law and He died under the law, and He satisfied every *jot and title* of the law (Matthew 5:17-18, Galatians 5:14, Luke 24:44) . It must be understood that the dispensation of Grace did not begin until after Christ sacrificial act on the Cross of Calvary was completed, and when He conquered death and rose from the grave 3 days and 3 nights later. It was first revealed to the Jews and then after they rejected the gospel message, Paul turned to the Gentiles (Acts 13: 45-46).

The Gospel records of Matthew, Mark, Luke and John recorded all that Christ did and said during these 3.5 years. In other words, the Nation of Israel and the Jews existed from when Abraham was called by God and will continue to exist until the end of this current age. God's statues and laws which were written on stone were replaced by a New Covenant in which God's laws were to be written on the heart. God established the Old Covenant with its laws and statutes after the Exodus from Egypt, and it continued until the death of Christ. After that point in time, the Old Testament laws and regulations which demanded salvation by works were replaced by love and grace. After the Jews and the spiritual leaders corporately rejected Jesus Christ as their long-awaited Messiah, God set aside the Jews and turned to the Gentiles (Acts 13:46). Israel was not abandoned...just set aside so that the Body of Christ could be formed during the church age. Salvation was now freely offered to Jews and Gentiles alike by faith, not by works of the law. Before the cross, there were only two classes of people...*Jews and Gentiles*. After the cross there are still only two classes of people.....*Christians and non-Christians.*

...in the midst of the week he shall cause the sacrifice and the oblation to cease, and for the overspreading of abominations he shall make it desolate Daniel 9:27

In the midst of the last week would be after approximately 3.5 years. We know that the earthly ministry of Christ lasted 3.5 years, and after that period of time he was *cut off* (Daniel 9:26)...crucified. When Jesus Christ died on the Cross of Calvary He said that: *It is finished*. The persecution and torture of the Messiah was finished....The Old Covenant was finished as a way to salvation...and the Levitical Sacrificial system for the atonement of sins was finished. Jesus Christ lay in the tomb for a full 3 days and 3 nights, and after 72 hours He arose from the dead. He had perfectly satisfied the Feast of Passover...He was the perfect sacrificial Lamb of God who was offered up to the Father for the permanent forgiveness of sin. He arose late on Saturday, Nisan 17 and early on the morning of Nisan 18 He ascended to the Father as a *Firstfruits Offering* on the Jewish Feast of Firstfruits. He was accepted by the Lord as a guarantee of a larger harvest to follow...Jews and Gentiles...under a New Covenant (Jeremiah 31:31). When Jesus Christ died and ascended to heaven as a Firstfruits offering, the Old Testament Levitical sacrificial system ceased to exist. The Old had passed away, and the New had come. Jesus said:

Behold, your house is left unto you ***desolate*** Matthew 23:38

Behold, your house is left unto you ***desolate****: and verily I say unto you, Ye shall not see me, until the time come when ye shall say, Blessed is he that cometh in the name of the Lord*
Luke 13:35

Grammatical Analysis

*And **he** shall confirm the covenant with many for one week: and in the midst of the week **he** shall cause the sacrifice and the oblation to cease, and for the overspreading of abominations **he** shall make it desolate, even until the consummation, and that determined shall be poured upon the desolate* Daniel 9:27

The identification of whether the personal pronoun in Daniel 9:27 is either the Antichrist or Jesus Christ. This issue has previously been addressed previously and it was determined that Jesus Christ is the correct choice. However, a large majority of prophecy scholars have adamantly insisted that it must be the Antichrist. Turning from a doctrinal or scriptural basis, let us examine the antecedent of the personal pronoun ***he*** and determine what is grammatically correct. A personal pronoun always modifies another personal pronoun or a previous antecedent noun. Therefore, in order to determine the antecedent of ***he*** in verse 27 we must look at verse 26.

And after threescore and two weeks shall Messiah be cut off, but not for himself: and the people of the prince that shall come shall destroy the city and the sanctuary; and the end thereof shall be with a flood, and unto the end of the war desolations are determined Daniel 9:26

The popular interpretation is that by the rules of grammar **he** must refer to a *prince that shall come* and that this must be the Antichrist (Of course, the word Antichrist never appears in the Old Testament...but we digress). Unfortunately, for all those English scholars who identify **he** with the ***prince*** that old dog won't hunt. *Prince* is grammatically the object of the preposition *of* in the phrase *of the prince*. *Of the prince* is a prepositional phrase which modifies the antecedent *people*. *Prince* is not a grammatically correct antecedent so we must look further. *People* in Verse 26 also cannot be the antecedent of ***he*** in Verse 27, because *people* is a plural noun and *he* is a singular pronoun. *For himself* is a prepositional phrase that modifies *Messiah*. *Messiah* is a stand-alone noun which is both singular and masculine, and *He* is both singular and masculine. The inescapable grammatical conclusion is the ***he*** in Daniel 9:27 must be the Messiah in Daniel 9:26.

What is to be accomplished by the Messiah ?

And he shall confirm the covenant with many for one week: and in the midst of the week he shall cause the sacrifice and the oblation to cease, and for the overspreading of abominations he shall make it desolate, even until the consummation, and that determined shall be poured upon the desolate Daniel 9:27

There are four things which will be accomplished by ***he***.

- He will confirm the covenant with many for one week (7 years)

- He will cause sacrifice and oblation to cease
- He will make it (Herod's Temple) desolate until the consummation
- That determined will be poured upon the desolate

There is nothing in Daniel 9:27 that conveys the notion of immediacy. There is no indication that these things would occur either at once or in close proximity to one another. However, in hindsight we now know that the first 3 things were fulfilled at the 1st advent of Christ. The 4th will continue from the death of Christ until the end of the Great Tribulation.

He will confirm the covenant with many for one week (7 years)

He will *confirm the covenant with many.* Note that there is a great difference in *confirming* a covenant and *initiating* a covenant. A covenant is basically a promise. If Christ confirmed a covenant, it must have been previously stated...and it was.

Behold, the days come, saith the LORD, that I will make a ***New Covenant*** *with the house of Israel, and with the house of Judah* Jeremiah 31:31

The House of Israel and the House of Judah refers to the fractured united Kingdom of King David and his son King Solomon that was ripped into two parts at the death of King Solomon. the Southern Kingdom was called Judah (Tribes of Judah and Benjamin) and the Northern Kingdom was called the Kingdom of Israel (The remaining 10 tribes). The New Covenant was confirmed and fulfilled by Jesus Christ when He died upon the Cross of Calvary.

[8] *For finding fault with them, he saith, Behold, the days come, saith the Lord, when I will make a new covenant with the house of Israel and with the house of Judah:*
[9] *Not according to the covenant that I made with their fathers in the day when I took them by the hand to lead them out of the land of Egypt; because they continued not in my covenant, and I regarded them not, saith the Lord.*
[10] *For this is the covenant that I will make with the house of Israel after those days, saith the Lord; I will put my laws into their mind, and write them in their hearts: and I will be to them a God, and they shall be to me a people:*
[11] *And they shall not teach every man his neighbor, and every man his brother, saying, Know the Lord: for all shall know me, from the least to the greatest.*
[12] *For I will be merciful to their unrighteousness, and their sins and their iniquities will I remember no more.*
[13] *In that he saith, A new covenant, he hath made the first old. Now that which decays and waxes old is ready to vanish away* Hebrews 8: 8-13

He will cause sacrifice and oblation to cease

Many fine biblical scholars have been deceived and declared that the ***he*** in Daniel 9:27 is the antichrist. This is because just before the last 3.5 years of the Great Tribulation begins, there will be a great world leader who will arise in Europe who will unify a 10 nation confederacy by waging war against 3 of the nations and defeating them all. He will then become the political and military leader of them all. He will then manage to do the impossible....he will then establish and initiate a covenant with Israel under which Herod's Temple will be rebuilt and Jewish worship and sacrifices will be reinstated. This will no doubt grieve and dishonor Christ. He declared upon the Cross that *it is finished*. How many times must He sacrifice Himself and shed His precious blood for the remission of sins...only once. When Christ died it was the fulfillment and end of the Old Testament sacrificial system. He was the perfect, spotless Passover Lamb that was slain for sin. His sacrifice was not an atonement (covering) for sin but destroyed the curse of sin forever. He was both the sacrificer (High Priest) and the sacrifice for the permanent forgiveness of sins. He put Satan to shame and held him up for public display when He arose from the dead. He had abolished physical and spiritual death forever.

[**1**] *For the law having a shadow of good things to come, and not the very image of the things, can never with those sacrifices which they offered year by year continually make the comers thereunto perfect.*
[**2**] *For then would they not have ceased to be offered? because that the worshippers once purged should have had no more conscience of sins.*
[**3**] *But in those sacrifices there is a remembrance again made of sins every year.*
[**4**] *For it is not possible that the blood of bulls and of goats should take away sins*
Hebrews 10: 1-4

[**14**] *For by one offering he hath perfected for ever them that are sanctified.*
[**15**] *Whereof the Holy Ghost also is a witness to us: for after that he had said before,*
[**16**] *This is the covenant that I will make with after those days, saith the Lord, I will put my laws into their hearts, and in their minds will I write them;*
[**17**] ***And their sins and iniquities will I remember no more.***
[**18**] *Now where remission of these is,* **there *is no more offering for sin*** Hebrews 10: 14-18

The rending of the veil marked the cessation of sacrifices through Christ's death (Leviticus 4:6, 17; 16:2, 15). There cannot be a covenant without sacrifice (Genesis 8:20, Genesis 9:17, Genesis 15:9, Hebrews 9:15). The prophecies concerning a New Covenant were confirmed and the New Covenant was established by only one blood sacrifice which would render all subsequent temple sacrifices useless. Yes...they did continue for 40 years until Herod's Temple was destroyed in 70 AD but they were meaningless and an insult to Christ.

He will make it (Herod's Temple) desolate until the consummation

When Christ died in 30 AD, the temple was spiritually destroyed.

[**16**] *Know ye not that ye are the temple of God, and that the Spirit of God dwelleth in you?*
[**17**] *If any man defile the temple of God, him shall God destroy; for the temple of God is holy, which temple ye are* I Corinthians 3: 16-17

God in His mercy gave Israel 40 more years to repent and accept His Son as their Lord and Savior. Except for a few called His *little flock* (Luke 2:32), all who never believed have died in sin. The Jewish temple will not be rebuilt until the great world leader that will arise will allow it to be constructed. This will mark the beginning of the end. When all of Israel believes that they are living in peace and safety the Satan will arise and the antichrist will break the covenant with Israel and invade Jerusalem. He will assault the city and the temple. 1/3 of all the city inhabitants will die and the other 2/3 will flee to the wilderness. The Jewish Covenant of Peace will become a Covenant of Death

Because ye have said, We have made a ***covenant*** *with death, and with hell are we at agreement; when the overflowing scourge shall pass through, it shall not come unto us: for we have made lies our refuge, and under falsehood have we hid ourselves* Isaiah 28:15

And your covenant with death shall be disannulled, and your agreement with hell shall not stand; when the overflowing scourge shall pass through, then ye shall be trodden down by it Isaiah 28:18
The new temple will be desecrated and lie desolate throughout the last 3.5 years of Daniel's 70th Week. The temple in Jerusalem will be Satan's seat of power and he will reign there for a time, time and a half-a-time. After 1367 days the *consummation* (end) of Satan will have fulfilled at the Battle of Armageddon and.....

That determined will be poured upon the desolate

The antichrist will have great power during the last half of the seventieth week. Christ said:

[**15**] *When ye therefore shall see the abomination of desolation, spoken of by Daniel the prophet, stand in the holy place, (whoso readeth, let him understand:)*
[**16**] *Then let them which be in Judaea flee into the mountains:*
[**17**] *Let him which is on the housetop not come down to take anything out of his house:*
[**18**] *Neither let him which is in the field return back to take his clothes.*
[**19**] *And woe unto them that are with child, and to them that give suck in those days!*
[**20**] *But pray ye that your flight be not in the winter, neither on the Sabbath day:*
[**21**] *For then shall be great tribulation, such as was not since the beginning of the world to this time, no, nor ever shall be* Matthew 24: 15-21

The *determined time* is at the end of the last 3.5 years of the Great Tribulation. The fate of Satan has long been prophesied at the end of this age, and *that determined* will result in His being destroyed at the Battle of Armageddon) end with his destruction (Daniel 11:25, Revelation 19: 11-21). The Wrath of God against Satan will reach its fulfillment when the 7th bowl is *poured out* upon the desolate; or better upon the *desolator*. Another acceptable translation is: *Even until complete destruction that is decreed is poured out on the one who makes desolate.* God's wrath is poured out on Satan, the antichrist, the false prophet and all who follow Satan to their complete destruction. This judgment and destruction of has already been decreed. It will happen, and it will happen just as prophesied by many prophets, by Jesus Christ and in the Book of Revelation. The Lord will return in triumph as King of Kings and Lord of Lords and put down man's rebellion and bring in the Millennium Kingdom (Revelation 19-20). Israel's rebellion will have finally ceased and a remnant will be saved as prophesied.

The phrase *for the overspreading of abominations* conveys a meaning that both the City of Jerusalem and the Holy Temple will be the object of abominations until the end. Because of the abominations committed by the Jews and the Jewish leadership against Jesus Christ, God would not only destroy the city and sanctuary (Daniel 9:25) in 70 AD, but its desolation will continue until the time of the *consummation determined* by God. This phrase is taken from Isaiah 10.

[23] *For the Lord GOD of hosts shall make a consumption, even determined, in the midst of all the land.*
[24] *Therefore thus saith the Lord GOD of hosts, O my people that dwell in Zion, be not afraid of the Assyrian: he shall smite thee with a rod, and shall lift up his staff against thee, after the manner of Egypt.*
[25] *For yet a very little while, and the indignation shall cease, and mine anger in their destruction* Isaiah 10: 23-25

The consummation will be when Satan is defeated at the Battle of Armageddon. The Assyrian is a title associated with the Antichrist (Pink, *The Antichrist*). When these 4 things come to pass, *that determined shall be poured upon the desolate. What does this phrase mean*? In examining the original Greek, this phrase could have just as well been translated as: *Even until the consummation and excision, divine wrath shall be poured on the desolate city, temple and people* (Benson Bible Commentary). The Temple and the City was destroyed in 70 AD by Titus and his Roman army; the Jews were scattered all over the known world; WW II brought death and persecution to millions of Jews and the Temple Mount has been taken over by the Muslims. Today, anti-Semitism is rampant. The City of Jerusalem has been rebuilt, but it is an abomination to God. Jesus looked over the City just before He was crucified and lamented:

Behold, your house is left unto you ***desolate****: and verily I say unto you, Ye shall not see me, until the time come when ye shall say, Blessed is he that cometh in the name of the Lord*
Luke 13:35

All of these things fell upon the Jews because they *knew not the time of thy visitation.*

[**41**] *And when he was come near, he beheld the city, and wept over it,*
[**42**] *Saying, If thou hadst known, even thou, at least in this thy day, the things which belong unto thy peace! but now they are hid from thine eyes.*
[**43**] *For the days shall come upon thee, that thine enemies shall cast a trench about thee, and compass thee round, and keep thee in on every side,*
[**44**] *And shall lay thee even with the ground, and thy children within thee; and they shall not leave in thee one stone upon another; because thou* ***knew not the time of thy visitation****.*
Luke 19: 41-44

Why All of The Confusion?

Many prophecy teachers will steadfastly maintain that the ***he*** in view here is the *Antichrist* in the Book of Revelation. This is based upon the prophecy that as the Church Age draws to a close, a coalition of 10 nations will arise in the European Theatre (Daniel 7: 19-26). They will unify as a group and control European activities. These nations will be formed out of the old Roman Empire. At the height of their power, a great economic and military figure will arise from among these 10 nations. He will supernaturally build a mighty political and military machine which will attack and conquer 3 of these 10 nations (Daniel 19:24). The remaining 7 nations will submit to this great world leader and he will gain control of the 10 nation confederacy and its military resources. He will then do something that cannot be imagined today: He will sign a Peace Treaty with Israel and somehow manage to grant authority to the Jews to rebuild Herod's Temple either on or near the old Temple Mount (Revelation 11: 1-2). The Jews will reinstate temple sacrifices and many will believe that this is their long awaited conquering King and Messiah. Little will they know that this is a Treaty of Death. In some unknown conflict, this great world leader will be slain with a sword or a knife (Revelation 13:1-4). As he lies in apparent death, Satan will raise him from the dead as part of God's divine plan. This individual will be completely taken over by Satan. He is who we call the Antichrist. After Satan is cast down to this earth (Revelation 12:9), He will invade Jerusalem and overthrow the rebuilt Temple. He will then desecrate the Temple and the Antichrist will sit in the temple declaring himself to be Jesus Christ (Matthew 24:15, Daniel 12:11). Those who will not bow down and worship him will be martyred (Revelation 13: 11-15).

*And **he** shall **confirm the covenant** with many for one week: and in the midst of the week **he** shall **cause the sacrifice and the oblation to cease**, and for the overspreading of abominations **he** shall **make it desolate**, even until the consummation* Daniel 9:27

This is the basis for saying that the ***he*** in Daniel 9:27 is the Antichrist. *First,* the text clearly says that this *he* is to *confirm a covenant for one week.* there is a great deal of difference in *confirming* a covenant and *establishing* a covenant. Jeremiah wrote: *Behold, the days come, saith the LORD, that I will make a New Covenant with the house of Israel, and with the house of Judah* (Jeremiah 31:31). Recall that the Hebrew word covenant can also mean *promise.*

The Antichrist never confirmed anything. He is the great deceiver and the father of lies. It was not the Antichrist that *confirmed the covenant with many for one week* (Daniel 9:27) but Jesus Christ. The deception that has been propagated by identifying the ***he*** in Daniel 9:27 was a necessity by those who teach a 7 year tribulation period. Practically all agree that Satan and the Antichrist cannot begin their reign of terror until after Satan is defeated in Revelation 12. *Where did this concept of a 7 year tribulation originate?* We have shown that the Great Tribulation will last for 3 ½ years and will be far more severe than anyone can imagine. So much so that if the Lord doesn't return to put an end to it, not a single human would survive (Matthew 24:22). There is no hint of a 7 year tribulation period anywhere in the Holy Bible or in the Book of Revelation. The root of this belief is certainly in the misinterpretation of who will *confirm the covenant*, but the belief that this period of time is 7 years runs deep.

The apostle Paul specifically wrote that Jesus Christ confirmed this covenant bty His sacrificial death.

[**16**] *Now to Abraham and his seed were the promises made. He saith not, And to seeds, as of many; but as of one, And to thy seed, which is Christ.*
[**17**] *And this I say, that the covenant, that was confirmed before of God in Christ, the law, which was four hundred and thirty years after, cannot disannul, that it should make the promise of none effect* Galatians 3: 16-17

It appears that ancient Jewish scholars misinterpreted Daniel 9:27 because they had no knowledge...no clue....that Jesus Christ would arrive to redeem all Jews. In fact, even His Apostles never fully realized that Christ would be crucified until the last few days of His life here on earth. This is strange because there were over 100 prophecies concerning Jesus Christ as the long-awaited Jewish Messiah. A few key prophecies are summarized below.

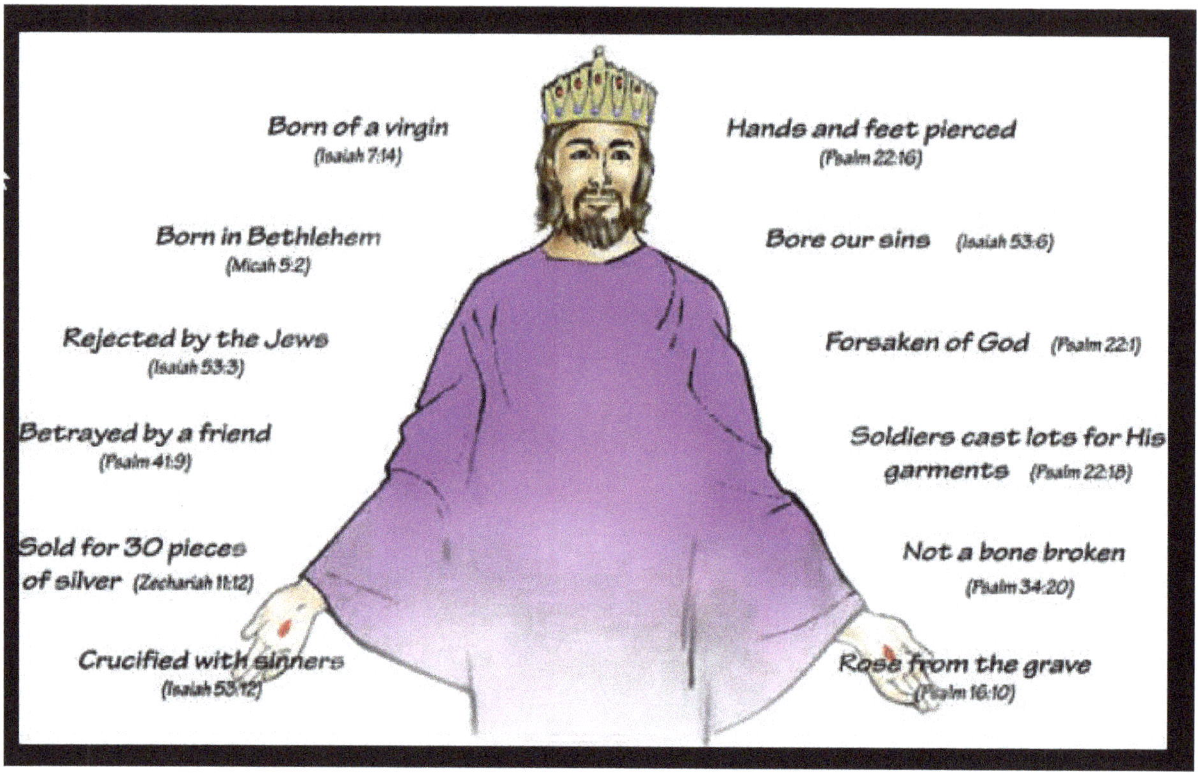

The prophets of old did reveal that He would be rejected by Jewish spiritual leaders and killed (*cut off*). After His crucifixion, God turned away from the Jews to the Gentiles to offer salvation to both Jews and gentiles based upon *faith and grace*. It had been prophesied by the prophets that a New Covenant was coming but they simply would not recognize such a thing. Hindsight is always better than foresight, and now that we have the New Testament, the New Covenant and the Book of Revelation... we can discern the truth. This is why studying the Bible as a Dispensational document is so important. When Christ was crucified and turned to the Gentiles God interrupted...but did not abandon...His plan to redeem and save Israel. The Jews could not do it...the law of Moses could not do it...and the Pharisees and Saducees could not do it. God had to send His only Son to live a sinless life under the law and then sacrifice his own perfect self to redeem sin. Freed from the law, Israel could now be saved only by faith and grace...not by the works of the law. We have already shown that when Christ arrived to preach redemption and repentance to the Jews there were certainly 7 years left in the Daniel blueprint for the salvation of the Jews. Christ went to the Jews and not the Gentiles for 3.5 years....He sent His disciples to the Jews and not the Gentiles...and He died so that salvation might come to Jews and Gentiles alike. A gap in time then had to take place during which the body of Christ would be formed under a New Covenant. Make no mistake about it, a Christian who has been baptized into Christ by the Holy Spirit is to save lost souls to Christ, but a major role of the church is to preach the gospel message to all Jews and turn them to Christ. This will continue until the 70th week of Daniel has run its course and the Battle of Armageddon will end the Age of Grace. This is serious business...Only faith in Jesus Christ as the only Son of God can save a person. The penalty for not doing so is eternal punishment in the Lake of Burning Fire. The Bible is not a book of generalities, it is a book of specifics and truth. The last 3.5 years of Daniels 70th week are still future and must take place to accomplish the 6 objectives of Daniel 9:24. . When you read the Bible literally and dispensationally there's no sense in which the last 3.5 years of Great Tribulation can be placed in the past. The last half of Daniel's 70th Week is the culmination of God's eternal plan for His chosen people when all Israel will be saved. That those who are seek wisdom understand.

The Gap Theory

When will the last week of Daniel begin and end? This question has been controversial for almost 2000 years. There are three theological positions. The *first* is that Daniel's 70th week will run consecutively from when it started, uninterrupted, for 490 years. The *second* is that the Daniel prophecy will be interrupted after 483 years and will not resume until the Great Tribulation begins. This will demand a 7 year tribulation period of time. The *third* position which this author has addressed is that the first half (3.5 years) of Daniel's 70th week was the ministry of Christ and the last half (3.5 years) represents the Wrath of Satan (The 7 Trumpet judgments) and the Wrath of God (the 7 Bowl judgments).

All "gap theorists" agree that the end of Daniels 490 years will end when the Great Tribulation ends. In this case, it is usually assumed that the 70 week prophecy of Daniel will end at the *Battle of Armageddon*. If Daniel's prophecy is interrupted either when Christ came to the River Jordan to be baptized or when He was crucified, when it will resume is a hotly debated topic. There are those who teach that the tribulation will be 7 years in duration, and that this time period constitutes the last complete (70th) week of Daniel. Another group will teach that the last 7 years of Daniel's prophecy will be composed of the 3.5 years ministry of Christ and the last 3.5 years will be a time of Satan's Wrath and the Wrath of God. *So who is right?....*

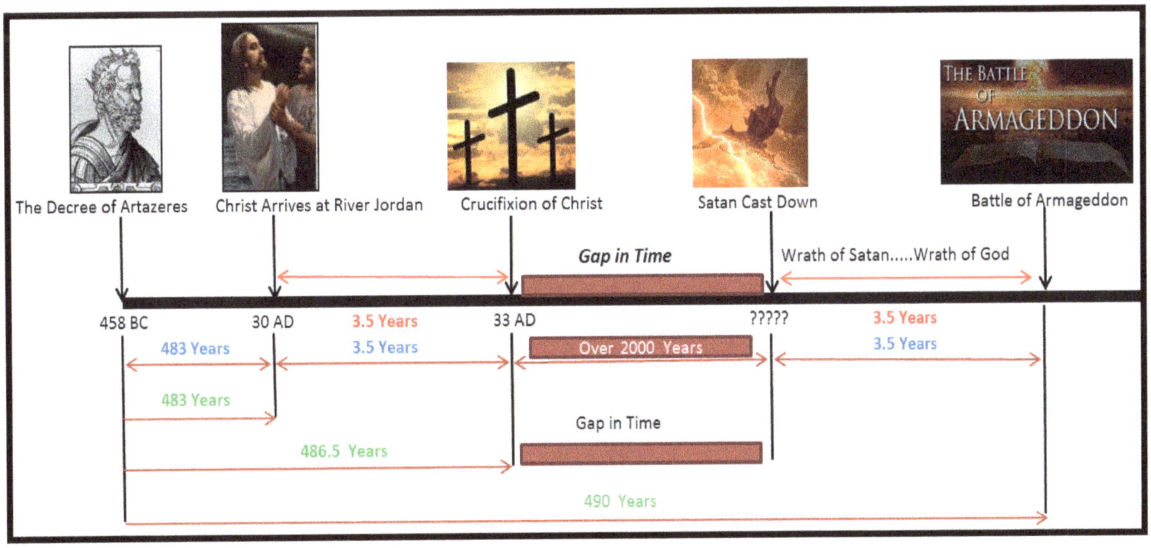

Obviously, either gap theory depends upon when the *first part* of Daniel's prophecy ends.

There is another group who propose that there is *no gap* in the 490 years, and they are in three camps. The 1st and most popular theory was proposed by the late Dr. John Walvoord, who assumed that the decree was issued by Cyrus in 448 BC and that the full period of 490 years expired in 33 AD (note that there is no zero year and when passing from 1 BC to 1 AD one must subtract one year. This has been the most popular interpretation of Daniel's 70 week prophecy because the Roman Catholic Church has decreed that Christ was crucified in 33 AD on a Friday. This rationale is not biblically sound. It ignores the fact that salvation will not come to the Jews corporately until the tribulation period forces them to turn to Christ as their true Messiah, and that the entire 70 weeks of Daniel are directed to the fate of God's chosen people...the Jews. Walvoord uses a 360 day prophetic year to support his calculations...an assumption challenged previously. The 2nd group who assert that there is *no gap* in the 490 years of Daniel claim that each year of the Daniel Prophecy is only 360 days long and that 490th year ends at the Crucifixion in 32 AD. Working backward from that date they claim that the decree to rebuild the temple and the city was issued in 445/444 BC decree by Artaxerxes I, Longimanus. This was first proposed by Sir Robert Anderson in an 1895 book called *The Coming Prince*. The 3rd group assumes that the decree which launched Daniels 70 week prophecy began in 457 BC and ended in 34 AD with the stoning of Steven. ALL of these positions fail to recognize that the Great Tribulation is dealing with the redemption and salvation of the Jews, and that the Daniel Prophecy is all about how God will restore His covenant with Israel. This cannot happen before the Great Tribulation comes to an end.. There is little or no biblical support for declaring a 360 day prophetic year and applying it to anything. God said exactly how long a year would be in Genesis 1:14. *And God said, Let there be lights in the firmament of the heaven ... and let them be for signs, and for seasons, and for days, and years"* Genesis 1:14

Using a 360-day year for interpretation of prophecy contradicts what the Bible specifies as the length of a biblical year, namely, the time it takes the Earth to go around the Sun. We know that this is 365.2422 days and the ancients knew it also (365 days). The pyramids in Egypt were built around a solar year; stone hedge in England was built around a solar year; and the ancient Maya had a perpetual calendar that was built upon a solar year. The solar year is necessary to accurately predict the seasons. Even the ancient Egyptians learned this . All adjusted their calendar to correct any inaccuracy. It must be stated again that God....who made the sun and moon to keep accurate track of time.... knew this from when they were created. He gave Moses the Jewish Lunar/Solar calendar at the Exodus so that they could observe His 7 annual feasts in *due time* . The assumption of a 360 day year consisting of 12 months is a fabrication necessary to shoehorn personal belief into biblical facts. Failure to include any of the future Great

Tribulation period in the restoration of Israel violates both the purpose of the Daniel prophecy and many Old Testament prophecies concerning the ultimate fate of the Jews.

It is concluded that there **must be a gap** in the Daniel Prophecy for one compelling reason. The 70 weeks of Daniel were directed to the Jews and only to the Jews. The bible is a book that was written by prophets of God under the inspiration of the Holy Spirit. All scripture is God inspired but it must be carefully studied and prayed over with the help of the Holy Spirit.

Study to shew thyself approved unto God, a workman that need not be ashamed, rightly dividing the word of truth II Timothy 2:15

The Daniel prophecy is a prime example of II Timothy 2:15. We have already pointed out multiple times that this prophecy is Jewish through and through. It reveals the ultimate fate of the Jews from the end of the 70 year Babylonian exile to the end of the Great Tribulation. Yes.....it does involve the Jewish Messiah and it does predict that war and persecution of the Jews would continue until *all of Israel will be saved. When will this happen?* At the end of the Great Tribulation. It has been stated by many well meaning expositors that there is no reason whatsoever to believe that there is a gap in time in this prophecy. This statement would be made by biblical Scholars who simply do not understand or accept the ultimate fate of the Jews. It has always been God's plan to commune with man as he did with Adam and Eve in the Garden of Eden. He chose Israel as His people.....His bride...His people to fulfill this plan. He promised (covenanted) with Abraham and told him that His *seed* would be blessed (plural) and that his *seed* (singular) would produce a Messiah who would redeem Israel. He promised to Abraham, Moses and King David that the Jews would someday inherit a promised land that would be divided among the 12 tribes of Israel. This is the primary purpose of the Millennial Kingdom. God promised King David that his seed would rule forever upon the Throne of David. He gave His word and He cannot lie...all of these things will come to pass. Because of their disbelief and because they crucified His Son the Jews have been *temporarily set aside....**Until When***? Until the church age is over...until the fullness of the Gentiles has come in.....and until the nation of Israel and the Jews will accept Jesus Christ as their Lord and Savior....as the Great tribulation draws to a close. In fact, the entire purpose of the Tribulation Period is to bring Israel and the Jews to Jesus Christ as their Lord and Savior. *Why did the Daniel 70 week prophecy not come out and say that this is the eternal plan of God?* It is because that the Church Age or the Age of Grace, was completely hidden from the Old Testament prophets and prophecy. It was a mystery not known in times past until it was revealed by Paul after the crucifixion of Christ.

*Now to him that is of power to establish you according to my gospel, and the preaching of Jesus Christ, according to the revelation of the **mystery**, which was **kept secret since the world began*** Romans 16:25

Once this is realized and once the word of God is *rightly divided*, not only is a gap in time understood...... it is demanded to fulfill God's plan for His chosen people.

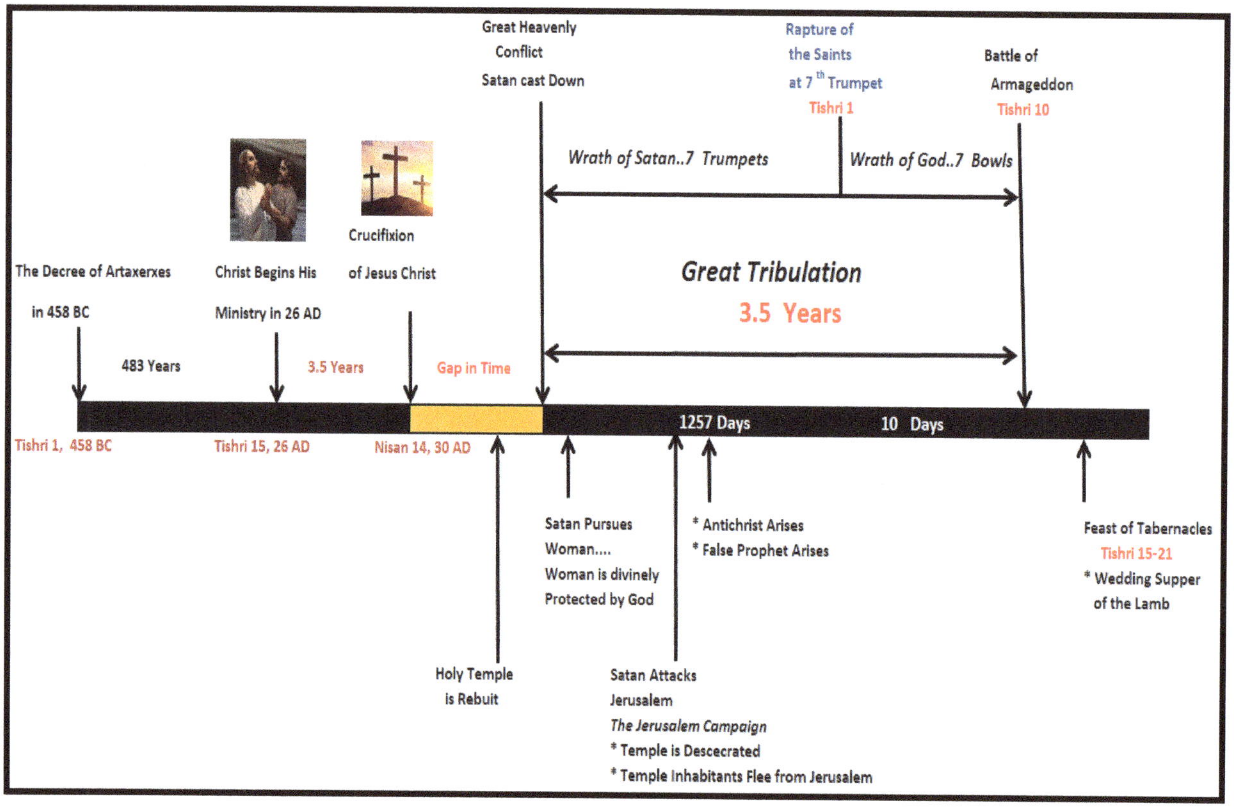

Daniel as A Dispensational Prophecy

Finally, the following observations are relevant to this issue (Kenneth I. Gentry, Jr., June 2005)

> The confirmation of the covenant mentioned in Daniel 9: 27 is woefully misunderstood by dispensationalists. According to Walvoord: "This verse of scripture refers to the coming world ruler at the beginning of the last seven years who is able to gain control over ten countries in the Middle East. He will make a covenant with Israel for a seven-year period. As Daniel 9:27 indicates, in the middle of the seven years he will break the covenant, stop the sacrifices being offered in the temple rebuilt in that period, and covenant and become their persecutor instead of their protector, fulfilling the promises of Israel's time of trouble (Jeremiah 30: 5–7)."

Several problems plague this interpretation, some of which have already been indicated previously.

1.0 The covenant here is not *made*; it is *confirmed*. This is actually the confirmation of a covenant already extant, *i.e.*, the covenant of God's redemptive grace confirmed by Christ (Romans 15:8).

2.0 The word *confirmed* is related to the name of the angel of God who delivered the message to Daniel: Gabriel (God is *strong*). The lexical correspondence between the name of the strong angel of God (who reveals the Seventy Weeks to Daniel) and the making strong of the covenant, suggest the predetermined confirmation of the covenant. Covenantal passages frequently employ related terms.

3.0 The parallelism with Daniel 9:26 indicates that the death of the Messiah is directly related to the confirming of the covenant. He is *cut off but not for himself* (Daniel 9: 26a). His confirmation is to the ancient prophets and to the Jews. He *confirms the covenant* for the "many" of Israel (Daniel 9:27a). His sacrificial death *brings* or *ratifies* the confirmation of the covenant, for *without shedding of blood there is no remission* (Hebrews 9:22).

4.0 The indefinite pronoun *he* does not refer back to the *prince who is to come of* Daniel 9:26. That "prince" is a subordinate noun and "the people" is the dominant noun. Thus, the misunderstood *he* refers back to the last dominant individual mentioned: who is *Messiah in Daniel 9:26a.* The *Messiah* is the prominent figure in the whole prophecy, and the destruction of the Temple is related to His death.
https://chalcedon.edu/resources/articles/daniels-seventy-weeks-and-biblical-prophecy

Conclusions

- The Daniel 70 week prophecy is a Jewish prophecy through and through
- The Daniel prophecy is Dispensational
- It reveals to Daniel the fate of his people which spans a period of time which is still ongoing and has been over 2400 years.
- The prophecy begins with a decree from Artaxerxes in his 7th year of reign, which authorized Ezra the Scribe to rebuild the temple, the walls and the City of Jerusalem in the fall of 458 BC.
- The prophecy refers to 70 weeks of years or 490 years (70x7) which are normal 365.2422 long as designed by God.

- The long awaited Jewish redeemer and Messiah who would redeem Israel from sin would arise after 483 years have elapsed. This would leave 7 years for the 70th week of Daniel

- *He* is not the Antichrist but he is Jesus Christ the Son of God. *He* will accomplish three things at His sacrificial death (Daniel 9:27).

  - he shall confirm the covenant with many for one week:

  - he shall cause the (temple) sacrifices and the oblations to cease

  - for the overspreading of abominations he shall make it (the temple) desolate

- In the middle of the last 7 years *He* will be *cut off* (killed, crucified), but *not for Himself*. *He* (Jesus Christ) died for the sins of the world...and in particular for the sins of all Israel and the Jews. The Old Covenant was finished, and the New Covenant began.

- The death of Jesus Christ was approximately 486.5 years into the 490 year prophecy.

- At this point, a *gap* in the Daniel prophecy began. It is of unknown duration, but the prophecy will begin again when Satan is cast down to the earth and the Great Tribulation begins. The Great Tribulation is the Wrath of Satan and the Wrath of God. It will last approximately 3.5 years.

- The Daniel Prophecy will end at the Battle of Armageddon

God will once again begin His covenant relationship with Israel. He will fulfill His Land Covenant with Abraham, Moses and King David. Those Believing Jews who are still alive and remain will populate the 1000 year Millennial Kingdom.

> [25] ***For I would not, brethren, that ye should be ignorant of this mystery, lest ye should be wise in your own conceits; that blindness in part is happened to Israel, until the fullness of the Gentiles be come in.***
> **[26]** ***And so all Israel shall be saved: as it is written, There shall come out of Zion the Deliverer, and shall turn away ungodliness from Jacob:***
> **[27]** ***For this is my covenant unto them, when I shall take away their sins***

Romans 11: 25-27

CHAPTER 2

The Decree That Initiated Daniels Prophecy

THE COMMANDMENT TO RESTORE THE TEMPLE AND REBUILD JERUSALEM

It is crucial that we determine exactly when the commandment to *restore and rebuild the City of Jerusalem went forth*. There are two basic things to consider. The *First* is that we are able to look back in time and determine the most likely time and place that this commandment occurred. *Second*, the decree which will initiate the 70 week prophecy of Daniel must lead to the *beginning* of the ministry of Christ when he came to the River Jordan to be baptized by John the Baptizer 483 years after the Decree went forth. Every Biblical scholar agrees that Christ was crucified between 30 AD - 34 AD. It has been established that Christ was born in 5 BC (Phillips, *The Birth and Death of Christ*) and that Christ was crucified in 30 AD (Phillips, *The Birth and Death of Christ; A Forensic Analysis, Phillips, The Birth of Christ,* Coulter, Fred R., *The Day Jesus Christ Died*). We will now show that these two dates can be confirmed by the Daniel prophecy. There are four possible decrees that must be considered.

THE DECREE OF CYRUS

In 539 BC, the Persian King Darius conquered Babylon and installed Cyrus (a Mede) to act as king. This happened after the prophet Daniel had completed about 67 years in exile, which had previously been prophesied by Jeremiah (Jeremiah 29:10). In Ezra 1:1 we read: *Now in the first year of Cyrus king of Persia, that the word of the Lord by the mouth of Jeremiah might be fulfilled, the Lord stirred up the spirit of Cyrus, king of Persia, that he made a royal proclamation.* This proclamation or decree authorized the return of Israel to Jerusalem to *build (rebuild) the house (temple) of the Lord.* From 539 BC, a span of 483 years *unto the Messiah the Prince* (Jesus Christ), would take us to 56 BC. This is way too early, so we must look elsewhere.

THE DECREE OF DARIUS

The rebuilding of the temple authorized by Cyrus did not go well. The *people of the land* (Ezra 4:4) resisted the project, and it is recorded in Ezra 4:24 that the work *ceased until the second year of the reign of Darius, king of Persia* **.** Darius succeeded Cyrus in 518 BC. The work had resumed in 520 BC under Haggai and Zechariah. The governor of the province surrounding Jerusalem came to the temple site and inquired: *Who hath commanded you to build this house?* (Ezra 5:3). They replied that King Cyrus had authorized the project. The governor then sent a letter to the king asking him to produce such a decree, if indeed one existed. A search was made and the original decree was found. Darius then reinforced this decree with one of his own. *Let the governor of the Jews and the elders of the Jews build this house of God in His place.* So Darius simply reissued and augmented the decree of Cyrus authorizing that the Temple of God be rebuilt. Based upon Ezra 4:24 and biblical/ archeological research, this event likely occurred in 520 BC. Again moving forward 483 years, we find an ending date of 37 BC. This was about when King Herod began to reign in Jerusalem, and is again much too early. We must search further.

The First Decree of Artaxerxes

In Ezra 7:1-10, we read that Ezra the scribe, who was a descendent of Aaron, approached King Artaxerxes I and petitioned the king to allow him and a band of Israelites to return to Jerusalem. Biblical scholars are in almost universal agreement that this occurred in either 458 BC or 457 BC. Ezra wanted to *set magistrates and judges* in place, *teach the laws of God,* and *let judgment be executed speedily,* upon all who would not obey the laws of God (Ezra 7). The petition was granted, and Ezra left *on the first day of the first month of Artaxerxes Seventh year,* and arrived in Jerusalem *on the first day of the Fifth month* (Ezra 7:9). We will later show that the decree went forth on *Tishri 14, 458 BC* and Ezra departed from the city of Babylon on Nisan 1 in 457 BC (Ezra 7:9). If the decree to Ezra was issued in 458 BC, and if the total elapsed years from 458 BC to the start of Christ ministry must be 483 years, we arrive at 26 AD. Please note that to arrive at 26 AD; we must subtract one year from a total of 484 years because when one crosses from BC to AD, there is no year zero. 26 AD is considered by many to be the year in which Jesus Christ came to the River Jordan and started his ministry of 3.5 years. This would demand that Christ was crucified in 30 AD. This is a strong candidate, but we will consider the final possible decree.

The Second Decree of Artaxerxes

In the 20th year of King Artaxerxes (Nehemiah 1:1) word came to Nehemiah that things were still not going so well in Jerusalem *The remnant that are left of the captivity there in the province are in great affliction and reproach. The wall of Jerusalem also is broken down, and the gates thereof are burned with fire* (Nehemiah 1:3). Nehemiah wept, mourned, fasted and petitioned God to turn the heart of Artaxerxes to let him go to Jerusalem and rebuild, for he was the King's personal cupbearer (Nehemiah 1:11; 2:1). God moved Artaxerxes' heart, and he gave Nehemiah permission to return. He also sent a letter to a merchant called *Asaph* informing him to supply timber to rebuild the gates, the walls and the temple (Nehemiah 2:6-8). This commission was issued to Nehemiah in the month of Nisan (Nehemiah 2:1).

Sir Robert Anderson

In 1882 Sir Robert Anderson published a book called *The Coming Prince.* In this book he determined that the month of Nisan in 445 BC must have been in the 20th year of Artaxerxes reign. Hence, Anderson declared that the decree was issued in the month of Nisan, 445 BC. After a four month trip to Jerusalem Nehemiah installed a judiciary and Daniels 70th week would start on Tishri 1, 445 BC. If we subtract 484 years from this date we would arrive at September of 39 AD. This is much too late for the death of Christ. At this point, Anderson made a rectifying assumption. Using the flood account of Gen 6-8, he declared based upon Genesis 7:11, 7:24 and 8:4 that a *prophetic month* was only 30 days long, and a *prophetic year* was 360 days long. He supported this theory by referring to the Book of Revelation, which equates 1260 days to 42 months (Revelation 11:2-3), ignoring the fact that the Book of Revelation would not be written until about 50-60 years after the crucifixion of Christ. Using a year as 360 days, he multiplied 360 days times 483 years. He then converted this number of prophetic days into a *Gregorian* calendar year, even though the Gregorian calendar would not be formed until 1582 BC. After adjusting for leap years, Newton arrived at Nisan 10, Psalm Sunday in 32 BC. The subsequent date for the crucifixion of Christ was then determined to be on Thursday, Nisan 14, in 32 AD. The 7 years remaining in Daniel's 490-year prophecy were then given to the tribulation period of John's Revelation. His results have been widely accepted since they were published, but it has been shown that many of his assumptions were flawed (http://www.pickle-publishing.com/papers/sir-robert-anderson.htm).

Harold Hoehner

The Roman Catholic Church has decreed for many centuries that Christ was crucified on Friday, Nisan 14 in 33 AD. To accommodate this date, Hoehner assumed that the month of Nisan in 444 BC must have been in the 20th year of Artaxerxes reign. Hoehner then assumed that the 70 weeks of Daniel commenced on Nisan 1, 444 BC. Using an approach similar to Isaac Newton, and using 360 day prophetic years, Hoehner arrived at Palm Sunday, Nisan 10 in 33 AD as his *terminus quo* of the first 483 years. He then declared that Friday, Nisan 14, 33 AD was the crucifixion date of Jesus Christ. Since the Roman Catholic Church dogmatically holds to a Friday crucifixion day, Hoehner's work has been widely accepted.

We can only applaud Sir Robert Anderson and Harold Hoehner for using such a clever approach to arrive at either 32 AD (Newton) or 33 AD (Hoehner) as a crucifixion year. Both dates have been widely acclaimed as correct by two large groups of followers. However, the basic assumptions and methods used by both Anderson and Hoehner have been critically assailed and claimed in error by Pickle, Ice and Jones to name a few. ***First***, the flood account in Genesis *does* state that over a period of 150 days, five months elapsed, but this does not guarantee that *each month* of the year was 30 days in duration or that a year was 360 days long. In fact, if anyone wants to carefully study the narrative in Genesis 7 & 8 they will find that from when Noah entered the ark until he left the ark was 365 days, and it could have been exactly one solar year of 365.2422 days which would imply a normal year. (Phillips, Noahs Ark: *Historical and Prophetic Truths*). ***Second***, the book of Revelation would not be written for about another 620 years, so Daniel would have no knowledge of that text. ***Third***, Daniel was nearing the end of the 70-year period of Babylonian exile when he received the prophecy. He was not experiencing 360-day prophetic years during his exile, but full solar years. He was also well aware that the 70 years of exile were almost over when he petitioned God in prayer and fasting. There would be no confusion whatsoever in associating *full solar years* with the 70 week prophecy given to Daniel (Daniel 9:24). ***Fourth***, if Daniel *understood* (Daniel 9:23) that the 490-year prophecy was *not* based upon the Babylonian calendar year or the Jewish calendar year, which was on the average very close to a modern solar year, there was certainly no indication of that in his conversation with Gabriel nor in the Biblical record. There is no hint or any divine revelation whatsoever that a 360-day *prophetic year* ever existed in the canon of Holy Scripture or after the Exodus from Egypt. In fact, to keep the Passover every year in the correct month at the correct time of year, a 360 year *could not* be in use. Of course, the 360 day year proponents never suggest that anything but a full solar year was in use following the exodus. They simply state with a great deal of confidence that the *360 year prophetic year* was a *mystery* hidden until Sir Isaac Newton discovered it! Finally, everyone today does have access to the book of Revelation, and there is no doubt that the last 3.5 years of the tribulation period *seems* to be 1260 days, and this seems to be equated to 42 months (Revelation 11:2-3). Ah ha! They say, Daniel was told this by Gabriel and he knew it all along. After all, Gabriel told Daniel that he would *understand*. This is *high conjecture* at best. In this author's opinion, the assumption of a 360-day *prophetic year* is simply unwarranted. The conclusion of the matter is that the only decree which makes logical sense, and fits all the requirements of a normal 490-solar year prophecy, is the one issued by Artaxerxes in either 457 BC or 458 BC. We will now show that 458 BC is indeed the correct year and that a full (365.2422 days) solar year is indicated.

After examining the available options, the commandment to restore and to rebuild Jerusalem (Daniel 9:25) which initiated the 70-week prophecy of Daniel is the decree from Artaxerxes I to the scribe, Ezra. Ezra left Babylon *on the first day of the first month* (Ezra 7: 1-9) . After gathering the people together and assembling a group of Levites to conduct temple services, he *departed from the River of A-Haya on the 12th day of the first month* (Ezra 8:31). He arrived in Jerusalem on the *first day of the 5th month.* Hence, the actual journey took about 3.5 months. Ezra left on the 1st day of first month and arrived on the 1st day of the fifth month in *Artaxerxes 7th year of reign*. There are three key questions: *when was Artaxerxes 7th year? What month was the 1st month? When did the decree go forth*? To determine the seventh regnal year of Artaxerxes, we need to discuss two fundamental and related issues. Artaxerxes was a Persian king: (1) *In what month of the year did Persian kings begin to count their regnal years?* (2) *How did Persian kings transition from the death of one king to the next?*

THE BEGINNING OF REGNAL YEARS

We will briefly review calendar systems used to mark time. Each ancient kingdom had their own calendar system which was used to determine the beginning of a king's reign. Each ancient kingdom employed a slightly different calendar, but most had learned that the length of a solar year and the time each season changed was determined by the sun; which we now know is exactly 365.2422 days. A calendar year was composed of 12 months and a week of seven, 24-hour days. All ancient societies used a basic 12 month year, but the number of days in each month varied from calendar to calendar, as did the actual number of total days in each year. The length of a month in ancient times was usually set at either 29 or 30 days. This is because the actual length of a lunar month is determined by the rotation of the moon around the earth, and is 29.53059 days. Calendars are designed to mark time by the passage of months, with the number and initiation of each month designed so that a series of months would exactly coincide with the solar year. The *basic* Hebrew calendar year is generally recognized as 12 months per year with alternating 29 and 30 day months. However, two consecutive, standard lunar months would be (2*29.53059)=59.1 days and over a 12 month period (59.51*6)=354.4 days. A standard solar year is 365.2422 days. Clearly, a Hebrew year of 12 alternating 29 and 30 day months would fall back against a standard solar year by about 11 days per year. There were two common solutions to the problem: the first was to add days during each year and to periodically add an extra (13th) month to the normal 12-month year. For example, the Egyptians used a simple 12-month calendar consisting of 12 months of 30 days per year. This would total to 360 days per year. They then added 5 days at the end of the

12th month, so that their year was 365 days. This was close to the actual solar year, but fell short about 0.25 days per year. Hence, the calendar *drifted backward* about one day every four years. It would continue to drift back through the solar year, so that after about 1460 years, the Egyptian year would move back in sync with a true solar year. For example, if today was Christmas using this calendar, in about 730 years Christmas would be in July!

The Jews needed a *Lunar-Solar* calendar. They had to accurately predict when a new moon would occur each month, and at the same time use a 365.25 day year to accurately track the seasons of planting and harvesting. The basic calendar consisted of 12 alternating 30 and 29 day months. Simple math shows that a Hebrew year was only 354 days, which is about 11.25 days short of a solar year. About every three years, the calendar would drift back approximately 33.75 days. To keep the lunar-based 12-month year in sync with the solar year, it was discovered that by adding seven extra months over a 19-year period of time and periodically adding or subtracting a day... 19 lunar calendar years of 12 or 13 months.... would almost exactly equal the solar calendar over the same period of time. This 19-year period of time with seven inter-calculated months is called a *Metonic cycle*.

This same Jewish calendar is still in use today. It must again be stressed that since the Seven Feasts of Israel were ordained by God, and were to be observed every year following agricultural cycles, the Hebrews after the exodus *had* to keep their 12-month lunar calendar in sync with the solar year. Each civilization had its own names for each month of the year, but after the 70-year Babylonian exile, the Hebrews adopted the Babylonian calendar names with only slight variations. The calendar we use today is called the *Gregorian Calendar*. It was derived from the *Julian Calendar*. The Gregorian calendar is very accurate. Mechanics of the Jewish calendar were revealed by Hillel II in 358 AD. The following table is a summary of the Julian, Gregorian, Babylonian and Hebrew calendars.

	Julian	*Gregorian*	*Hebrew*	*(Civil)*	*Babylonian*	
Month	*Name*	*Name*	*Name*	*Months*	*Name*	*Months*
1	*Januarius*	*Jan*	*Tishri*	*Sept/Oct*	*Nisanu*	*Mar/Apr*
2	*Februarius*	*Feb*	*Heshvan*	*Oct/Nov*	*Aiaru*	*Apr/May*
3	*Martius*	*Mar*	*Chislev*	*Non/Dec*	*Simanu*	*May/Jun*
4	*Aprilus*	*April*	*Tebeth*	*Dec/Jan*	*Duzu*	*Jun/July*
5	*Maius*	*May*	*Shevat*	*Jan/Feb*	*Abu*	*July/Aug*
6	*Junius*	*June*	*Adar*	*Feb/Mar*	*Ululu*	*Aug/Sept*
7	*Julius*	*July*	*Nisan*	*Mar/Apr*	*Tashritu*	*Sept/Oct*
8	*Augustus*	*Aug*	*Iyyar*	*Apr/May*	*Arahsamnu*	*Oct/Nov*
9	*Septembris*	*Sept*	*Sivan*	*May/Jun*	*Kislimu*	*Non/Dec*
10	*Octobris*	*Oct*	*Tammuz*	*Jun/July*	*Tebetu*	*Dec/Jan*
11	*Novembris*	*Nov*	*Ab/Av*	*July/Aug*	*Shabatu*	*Jan/Feb*
12	*Decembris*	*Dec*	*Elul*	*Aug/Sept*	*Addaru*	*Feb/Mar*

*Before the Exodus from Egypt, *Tishri 1* began a Hebrew *Civil* year. After the Exodus, God ordained that every year would begin on *Nisan 1* to commemorate their being freed from Egyptian slavery. Hence, all references to "Month 1" *before* the Exodus referenced Tishri 1, and *after* the exodus it was Nisan 1. Egyptian years always began on a month called *Thoth 1*. The Julian Calendar date of Thoth 1 for any BC year can be calculated using modern computers. It "drifts" back across Julian months at a rate of about 1 day every 4 years.

After the Medo-Persia empire overthrew the Babylonian empire in 539 BC, the Persian Empire also adopted the Babylonian calendar for their own use. The Babylonians, Hebrews and Persians all used a common method for determining when a king came to reign. The Babylonians, Persians and Hebrews all used *Tishri 1* (September/October). the Egyptians used a month called *Thoth* 1(December). This was proved and published by Horn and Wood based upon earlier work by Thiele and is now widely accepted. Babylonian calendar years started on Nisan 1. The Hebrews used two new year days. Their *religious years* started on Nisan 1 and their *civil years* started on Tishri 1.

How Was the Reign of Ancient Kings Determined ?

Before we proceed, it is necessary to define how ancient kings counted their years of reign. Every civilized nation had a calendar that was used to keep track of time and started at a particular time of year. The reign of each king in every nation did not always coincide with the yearly calendar start month. It is believed that the Hebrew calendar came into existence from God to Moses at the time of the Exodus. This was because God commanded Israel to observe the New moons and His 7 holy feasts at exactly the same time each year. It is conjectured that the Babylonians adopted the basic Jewish Calendar and by the 5th century BC they were almost identical. Both started each month on a New Moon and tracked the seasons with an average year of 365.25 days. The Babylonian calendar began each year on Nisan 1 (March/April). The Hebrews originally started each year on Tishri 1 (September/October), but after the Jewish exodus from Egypt God declared that the 7th month known as Nisan would begin each year to commemorate the exodus. This did not affect the passage of time, it simply rotated the numbering of each month. Rather than completely abandon their old Tishri 1 new years day, the Jews declared that there would be a *Spiritual year* which would start on Nisan 1 (March/April) and that there would be a *Civil year* that would start on Tishri 1 (September/ October). The regnal years of Judah after the divided kingdom started on Tishri 1.

Every nation had a King, and the reign of kings would be recorded as *actual years* or *regnal years* (credited years of reign). Fortunately, when Artaxerxes I was reigning both Israel and Babylonian Kings had the same coronation day from which credited years of reign were determined...that was on Tishri 1 (September/October). There were two systems in use to determine how many credited years of reign that a king could claim from when he ascended to the throne. ...an *accession year* system and a *non-accession* year system. Suppose that King Don started his 5th year of reign on Tishri 1, September 15 in 500 BC, and he was killed in battle on Adar 10, March 2, 499 BC. King John succeeded King Don and assumed the throne on Adar 11, March 3. In an *accession year* system, all of the months between Tishri 1 in 500 BC and Tishri 1, 499 BC would be counted as the reign of King Don and not King John. The 5th and last year of King Don would be Tishri 1, 500 BC to Tishri 1, 499 BC. The 1st regnal year of King John would not begin until Tishri 1 (September/October), 499 BC even though he assumed the throne on March 3, 499 BC (accession year system). One might think of the actual reign of King John between March 2, 499 BC and Tishri 1 (September/Oct), 499 BC as Year 0. In a *non-accession* year system, King Don would still be credited with a full 5 year reign (Tishri 1, 500 BC-Tishri 1, 499 BC) , but King John's 1st year of reign would be counted as a full year between March 3, 500 BC and Tishri 1, 499 BC. The non-accession year system could and usually did create havoc when recording historical events. For example, if King John won a major battle on March 30, 499 BC would it be recorded in the 5th year of King Don or in the 1st year of King John or both if a non-accession year system was in use. When a king died during his reign, the Persians and Babylonians credited the entire year as his last year of reign, even if he died at the beginning of that year and his successor ruled for 11 months. In that case, the 1st 11 months of reign for the new Assyrian or Babylonian king would be called his *accession year* and credited to the old king. The credited reign of the new king would not start until the 1st day of the following regnal year. This is an *accession year* system or a *post dating* system. If a non-accession year system was in use, both the old king and the new king would be credited with an overlapping full 11 months of reign. This seems to be insane record keeping, but it was used because every ancient king wanted to be remembered as reigning over the maximum number of years possible.

The great biblical scholars Thiele, Horn and Wood proved that both the Persian and Babylonian Kings used the *accession* year system and so did the Hebrews after the fall of the Northern Kingdom of Israel in 723 BC. He also proved that both the Hebrews and the Persians/Babylonians used a *Tishri 1* (Sept/Oct) *inauguration day for each year of a King's reign*. Both the Hebrews and the Babylonians used essentially the same method to begin and end a king's reign. The Babylonians started each year on Nisan 1.

Hebrews in 5th Century BC	Persians/ Babylonians in 5th Century BC
* Started calendar Civil Year on Tishri 1	* Started Calendar Year on Nisan 1
* Started Religious calendar Year on Tishri 1	* Started official yearly reign of Kings on Tishri 1
* Started official yearly reign of Kings on Tishri 1	* Used an Accession Year system
* Used an Acession Year System	

The Reign of Artaxerxes I

From Ezra 7:9a, we know that Ezra left Babylon in the seventh year of Artaxerxes I reign, on the 1st day of the 1st month, but the Biblical record is silent in recording any *calendar year* or the *name* of the *first month*.

> *...in the reign of Artaxerxes, King of Persia, the King granted him all his requests... This Ezra went up from Babylon.... for upon the first day of the first month began he to go up from Babylon... In the 7th year of Artaxerxes the King* Ezra 7: 6-9

Ezra was a Hebrew who was writing for his own Jewish people, but he was in Persian/Babylonian exile. *So there is a scholarly debate as to which 1st month he used.* Was the 1st month on which Ezra left Babylon Tishri or Nisan? There is a valuable clue in the Book of Ezra. In Ezra 7:8, Ezra writes that *he arrived in the 5th month of the Kings 7th year of reign.* If we could accurately determine the 1st official year of Artaxerxes reign, we could easily determine the 7th year of his reign. We will shortly show beyond any doubt that the king who issued the decree was Artaxerxes I and that his 7th year of reign was 458 BC - 457 BC.

Ezra and Nehemiah were Hebrew contemporaries, and at least according to some sources the biblical records of both Ezra and Nehemiah were originally one document and that both must have referenced Persian events using Hebrew dating schemes. Whether that is true or not, the book of Nehemiah as it now stands clearly indicates that Nehemiah cross referenced Persian events to a Hebrew Tishri 1-Tishri 1 Civil calendar year, and *NOT* the Nisan-Nisan calendar year of Babylon (compare Nehemiah 1:1 to Nehemiah 2:1). If Nehemiah and Ezra were originally one document, the problem would be solved. However, no reliable data exists to prove or disprove this theory. Pragmatically, Ezra and Nehemiah were both serving in the King's court, and both were likely good friends; but this only suggests that both would use the same system to reference the reign of each king. Depending upon which system is being used by Ezra, the seventh year of Artaxerxes could be off by one year. Hence, imminent scholars are divided upon exactly when Ezra left Babylon in the7th year of Artaxerxes reign. Some defend a 458 BC date and some dogmatically defend a 457 BC date. *So which is to be believed?*

The critical issues are: *When was the 7th year of Artaxerxes reign?* and *When was the 1st month in Ezra 6:9?* The debate over whether Ezra and Nehemiah used a Babylonian system or a Hebrew system or when years start does not seem to be anything but a theological issue. In reality, what is important is *when* Artaxerxes who was in Babylon issued the decree to allow Ezra to return to Jerusalem. Artaxerxes was definitely using a Babylonian calendar and so we will only use that calendar to determine when the decree to Ezra was issued.

[6] *This Ezra went up from Babylon; and he was a ready scribe in the law of Moses, which the LORD God of Israel had given: and the king granted him all his request, according to the hand of the LORD his God upon him.*
[7] *And there went up some of the children of Israel, and of the priests, and the Levites, and the singers, and the porters, and the Nethinims, unto Jerusalem, in the seventh year of Artaxerxes the king.*
[8] *And he came to Jerusalem in the fifth month, which was in the seventh year of the king.*
[9] *For upon the first day of the first month began he to go up from Babylon, and on the first day of the fifth month came he to Jerusalem, according to the good hand of his God upon him*
Ezra 6: 6-9

Nebuchadnezzar was king over Babylonia...He was actually a Persian appointed king...and to restate known facts he was living under a calendar which started each calendar year on Nisan

1(March/April) and the reign of each king on Tishri 1 (September/October) . The Babylon Kings used an *accession* year system to determine how one king transitioned to the next....actual rein could start anytime after the death of a previous king but credited years always started on the first Tishri 1 after the death of the previous King.

The 7th Year of Artaxerxes Reign

The 70 week prophecy of Daniel (490 years) revealed that the Messiah would appear after 483 years had passed from when Ezra was given a decree from the king to return to Jerusalem. Almost every biblical scholar has Christ beginning His 3.5 years of ministry in the month of September /October in the month of Tishri. If 483 solar years were to fully pass until He arrived at the River Jordan in 26 AD, it is obvious that the decree *must* have been issued in September/October in 458 BC.... (458+26-1)=483 years. We have already shown that this king must have been Artaxerxes I. Ezra left for Jerusalem in the 5th month of his 7th year of his reign (Ezra 7:9a) and he arrived in the 5th Month of the 7th year of his reign.

[8] **And he came to Jerusalem in the fifth month, which was in the seventh year of the king.**
[9] *For **upon the first day of the first month began he to go up from Babylon**, and on the first day of the fifth month came he to Jerusalem, according to the good hand of his God upon him* Ezra 7: 8-9b.

This means that if the 7th year of Artaxerxes credited reign was Tishri 1, 458 BC - Elul 29, 457 BC, his 1st year of reign must have been Tishri 1, 464 BC - Elul 29, 463 BC. Sound exegesis of this logic must prove...or at least present sound evidence..... that this is true.

The most acceptable solution is to carefully examine historical and archeological records to determine when Artaxerxes began his 1st year of reign, and when he issued the decree to Ezra in the seventh year of Artaxerxes. We are quite certain that a Persian King named *Xerxes* preceded Artaxerxes. Xerxes was the biological father of Artaxerxes. It is also known that the Persian King Xerxes was assassinated in 465 BC and all historical records record that Xerxes is known to be the Babylonian King for 21 years, between 486 BC and 465 BC. He was reigning in Babylon during the ministry of both Ezra and Nehemiah. The main source for what actually took place during his last year of reign is attributed to an extensive study by a Historical Research Committee of 11 biblical scholars in 1945. Two of the members on this committee were S. H. Horn and L. H. Wood, who later studied over 100 ancient documents and in 1953 (updated in 1970) published a book called: *The Chronology of Ezra 7.* Much of the following material was derived from their work.

We are quite certain that a Persian King named Xerxes preceded Artaxerxes. It is also certain that King Xerxes was assassinated in 465 BC. There are two different accounts of His murder from ancient documents. The controversy surrounds *when* the assassination took place.

Regardless of when the assassination took place, Xerxes was murdered by a powerful courtier of his court called *Artabanus* who wanted to usurp the king. He then had the brother of Artaxerxes assassinated, and also tried to assassinate Artaxerxes. But, his plan was discovered and Artabanus was then killed by Artaxerxes. No record has ever been found that credits Artabanus as a reigning king of Persia, but a second-century historian called Mantheo wrote that a power struggle did indeed take place between Artabanus and Artaxerxes. However, Mantheo wrote his comments more than 500 years after the fact.

There have been two different scenarios which have been set forth. The *first* is that Artabanus assassinated Xerxes in early August of 465 BC. Xerxes had two sons who were heir-apparent. The oldest and crown prince was *Darius*. Artabanus went to Artaxerxes and told him that Darius had murdered his father so that he could ascend to the throne. To avenge his father, Artaxerxes arranged to have Darius killed. Artabanus now only had one man standing between him and the throne.....Artaxerxes. Artabanus then made plans to assassinate Artaxerxes, but a friend came to Artaxerxes and told him of the evil plot. Artaxerxes then killed Artabanus with a knife. Now consider the timeline. If Xerxes was murdered in early August, then Darius would immediately ascend to the throne as crown prince. If Darius was killed by Artaxerxes *before Tishri 1* he would not be a recognized king because he never ruled past the regnal start date of Tishri 1, 465 BC. Upon his death Artaxerxes would ascend and begin his 1st year of reign only a short time later on Tishri 1 . The short time between the death of Darius and the ascension of Artaxerxes would be the "accession year" of Artaxerxes. The official 1st year of Artaxerxes reign would be Tishri 1, 465 BC to Tishri 1, 464 BC. This would result in his 7th year of reign between 459 BC - 458 BC as shown in the Tishri table above.

	Tishri 1 Start Date
Year	
1	Tishri 1, 465 BC - Elul 29, 464 BC
2	Tishri 1, 464 BC - Elul 29, 463 BC
3	Tishri 1, 463 BC - Elul 29, 462 BC
4	Tishri 1, 462 BC - Elul 29, 461 BC
5	Tishri 1, 461 BC - Elul 29, 460 BC
6	Tishri 1, 460 BC - Elul 29, 459 BC
7	Tishri 1, 459 BC - Elul 29, 458 BC
8	Tishri 1, 458 BC - Elul 29, 457 BC
	Tishri 1 (Sept/Oct)

If Darius was not murdered until after Tishri 1, he would be credited with one year of reign even if he reigned just one day! But, there are no known historical documents or official records which credit Darius with ever reigning as king. In any case, Artabanus could never reign as king as long as Artaxerxes was still alive. The real problem is that if Darius was killed and if Artaxerxes assumed the throne before the end of August, 465 BC....then his 1st year of official, credited reign would begin on Tishri 1, 465 BC as shown above. 483 full years must elapse between the decree was issued by Artaxerxes to Ezra, and the arrival of Christ to be baptized by John the Baptist. Every prophecy teacher is certain that Christ came to the River Jordan in had to depart in the September/October. This means that the decree must have been issued in September/October. We are certain that Artaxerxes left on the *1st day of the 1st month*. This could not be on Tishri 1 because Artaxerxes was not King until Tishri 1. *What about Nisan 1*? This is impossible, since Nisan 1 is in March or April, and Ezra would need to depart after Tishri 1, 458 BC which would be in the 8th year of Artaxerxes reign. it should now be realized that the only 7th year of Artaxerxes which is possible to satisfy all requirements is Tishri 1, 458 BC to Elul 29, 457 BC. This could only be true if Artaxerxes assumed the throne *after* Tishri 1, 465 BC. Since this must be true, something unusual must have happened...and it did! As far as I can tell, no one has ever discussed this dilemma in any detail.

The 2nd scenario that will be proposed is that Xerxes was *not* assassinated in August of 365 BC but was murdered in early December of 365 BC, several months later. The accession year of Artaxerxes would be from when Darius the son of Xerxes was killed by Xerxes. Note almost all chronologists list 465 BC as Xerxes last year...which would be true in either case. Why would one choose to believe this second scenario? *Is there any evidence that Xerxes survived until December of 365 BC and received credit for the last year of Tishri 1, 465 BC - Tishri 1, 464 BC?* The possibility that Xerxes' death did not occur much earlier than December 1, 465 BC rests upon a famous double-dated document written in Egypt on January 1/2, 464 BC called ***AP 6***. This document bears the following date line: "on the 18th of Kislev, in the Egyptian month of Thoth, in year 21 (Reign of Xerxes) was when King Artaxerxes *began to sit* upon the throne. Thoth was the 1st month of the Egyptian calendar and it is equated with Kislev 18 which was December 7 in 465 BC. This document also contains information that clearly establishes that it was written in the *accession year* of Artaxerxes I. Unfortunately, the day number of the month Thoth is broken. The digits of that number could be restored to 7, 14, or 17 on paleographic grounds, but only the 17th of Thoth harmonizes with the 18th of Kislev and the proposed death of Xerxes. The 17th of Thoth fell on January 2/3, 464 BC, sunrise to sunrise. It is thus clear that by January 2, 464 BC, the news of Artaxerxes' accession had reached Egypt. It appears that the scribe of AP 6, having been in the habit of dating documents in the 21st year of Xerxes for several months, started out to do this and then finished the date line by adding the year of Artaxerxes' accession (Horn and Wood, *The Chronology of Ezra 7*). Although the actual death date of Xerxes will probably never be known, it is virtually certain that his death occurred near the end of the year in the month of December, 465 BC. By January 1/2, 464 BC the news of Artaxerxes accession to the throne had reached Egypt.

Horn and Wood provide other supporting evidence that the 2nd scenario concerning the death of Xerxes is correct. Another December date for the death of Xerxes comes from a cuneiform tablet found in an excavation of Ur in the Chaldees in 1930-1931. The tablet, which was uncovered in an archeological evacuation, was an agreement among four brothers who were dividing one section of land into four pieces. The agreement is dated in the 13th year of Artaxerxes I, but states that the original land division was signed in the Babylonian month of

Kislimu (November/December) in the 21st year of Xerxes. In that year Kislimu began, (according to the Parker-Dubberstein tables), on December 17. This document, along with the double - dated papyrus from the Jewish settlement of Elephantine in Egypt, can be used to confidently state the following conclusions.

- Xerxes was not assassinated until sometime in early December, 465 BC
- His death was rapidly followed by that of Darius and the usurper Artabanus
- The news of Xerxes death had not reached Egypt until late 465 BC (Horn and Wood) and the scribe in Elephantine wrote that Artaxerxes was in his *accession year* on January 1/2 in 464 BC.
- The last credited year of reign for Xerxes would be Tishri 1, 465 BC to Elul 29, 464 BC by the accession system. The accession "year" of Artaxerxes would be from the death of Xerxes in December of 465 BC to Tishri 1 in 464 BC.
- On Tishri 1, 464 BC Artaxerxes began his 1st day of official reign.
- The 7th year of Artaxerxes would begin on Tishri 1, August 28, 458 BC (Prolyptic date on Gregorian Calendar). The decree that authorized Ezra to return to Jerusalem would be *after* His 7th year had started. We will show in Chapter 3 that it was ***likely issued to Ezra*** on Tishri 19, September 15, 458 BC.

Regnal Years of Artaxexes I	
Year	
1	Tishri 1, 464 BC - Elul 29, 463 BC
2	Tishri 1, 463 BC - Elul 29, 462 BC
3	Tishri 1, 462 BC - Elul 29, 461 BC
4	Tishri 1, 461 BC - Elul 29, 460 BC
5	Tishri 1, 460 BC - Elul 29, 459 BC
6	Tishri 1, 459 BC - Elul 29, 458 BC
7	Tishri 1, 458 BC - Elul 29, 457 BC
8	Tishri 1, 457 BC - Elul 29, 456 BC
9	Tishri 1, 456 BC - Elul 29, 455 BC
10	Tishri 1, 455 BC - Elul 29, 454 BC
11	Tishri 1, 454 BC - Elul 29, 453 BC
12	Tishri 1, 453 BC - Elul 29, 452 BC
13	Tishri 1, 452 BC - Elul 29, 451 BC
20	Tishri 1, 445 BC - Elul 29, 444 BC

- Ezra would be leaving Babylon forever, and it would likely take him sometime to assemble his personal belongings, gather Jews from other tribes and persuade some of the Levitical priesthood to return to Jerusalem (Ezra 8-9).
- Ezra ***left*** Babylon on the 1st day of the 1st month and ***arrived*** in Jerusalem on the 1st day of the 5th month....in the 7th year of Artaxerxes. This cannot be on Tishri 1, 458 BC because the decree issued prior to Tishri 1 would not be in year 7. This leaves only one possible alternative: Ezra must have left on Nisan 1, March 21 (Gregorian) in 457 BC and arrived in Jerusalem on Av 1, July 17 five months later. His actual journey to Jerusalem took a little over 4.5 months (Ezra 8:31). Note that all of these things were in the 7th year of Artaxerxes reign as required.

- The 7th year of Artaxerxes between Tishri 1, 458 BC and Elul 29, 457 BC is the *only* year that satisfies all the requirements.

We now have determined that:

7	**Tishri 1, 458 BC - Elul 29, 457 BC**

- The last year of Xerxes reign was Tishri 1, 465 - Elul 29, 464 BC.
- The first year of Artaxerxes reign was Tishri 1, 464 BC - Elul 29, 463 BC. The 7th year of Artaxerxes reign was 458 BC - 457 BC.

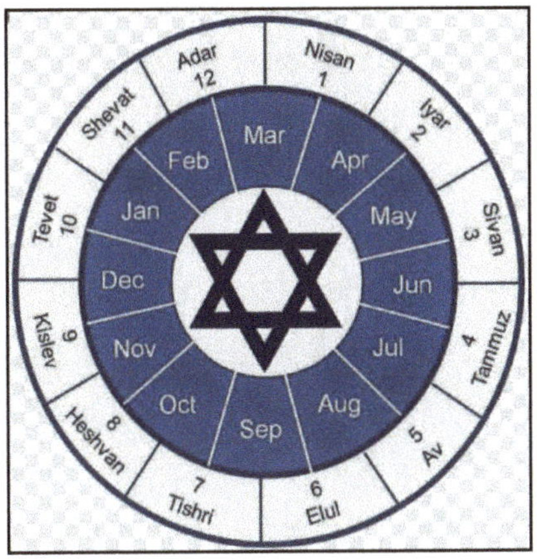

- Xerxes was murdered in December, 465 BC and not in August of 465 BC. September 1, 465 BC - Elul 29, 464 BC was his 21st year of credited reign.
- By December 17, 465 BC Darius had also been murdered.
- Artabanus was killed by Artaxerxes before January 1/2, 464 BC.
- The double-dated Egyptian Elephantine document AP 6 and the Tablet recovered from Ur both testify that by January 1/2, 464 BC Artaxerxes was in his accession year.
- Artaxerxes 1st year of official reign began on Tishri 1, 464 BC and ended on Elul 29, 463 BC. The 7th year of his reign began on Tishri 1, 458 BC and ended on Elul 29 in 457 BC.
- Ezra *received permission to return to Jerusalem* on Tishri 19 in 458 BC, 19 days after His 7th year of reign began on Tishri 1. This will be shown in Chapter 3
- Ezra left Jerusalem on Nisan 1, March 21 in 457 BC and arrived in Jerusalem on Av 1, July 17 (Gregorian prolyptic date) in 457 BC.
- Ezra left Babylon and arrived in Jerusalem in the 7th year of Artaxerxes reign as required.

Regnal Years of Artaxexes I	
Year	
1	Tishri 1, 464 BC - Elul 29, 463 BC
2	Tishri 1, 463 BC - Elul 29, 462 BC
3	Tishri 1, 462 BC - Elul 29, 461 BC
4	Tishri 1, 461 BC - Elul 29, 460 BC
5	Tishri 1, 460 BC - Elul 29, 459 BC
6	Tishri 1, 459 BC - Elul 29, 458 BC
7	Tishri 1, 458 BC - Elul 29, 457 BC
8	Tishri 1, 457 BC - Elul 29, 456 BC
9	Tishri 1, 456 BC - Elul 29, 455 BC
10	Tishri 1, 455 BC - Elul 29, 454 BC
11	Tishri 1, 454 BC - Elul 29, 453 BC
12	Tishri 1, 453 BC - Elul 29, 452 BC
13	Tishri 1, 452 BC - Elul 29, 451 BC
20	Tishri 1, 445 BC - Elul 29, 444 BC

The astute reader might have noticed something unusual.
The 1st month in the Babylonian calendar year is Nisan, and the 1st month of the Jewish

religious year is also Nisan 1. Therefore, the departure date from Babylon and the arrival date in Jerusalem synchronizes with both the Babylonian and the Hebrew calendar. Everything fits like a glove.

The Arrival of Messiah 483 Years After the Decree of Artaxerxes

It is demanded that If the 490 year prophecy of Daniel began in September of 458 BC when Artaxerxes issued a decree to Ezra allowing him to return to Jerusalem, then Christ started his ministry in the September of 26 AD, 483 Hebrew calendar years will elapse between these two points in time (483+26-1) = 483 years. Note that 1 year must be subtracted from the calculated time span of (483+ 26 years) because there is no year zero when crossing from BC to AD. It is certain that Ezra arrived in Jerusalem on the 1st day of the 5th month in the 7th regnal year of Artaxerxes reign (Ezra 7:9). Ezra left Babylon in the fall of 458 BC and arrived in Jerusalem 5 months later, *both* in the 7th year of Artaxerxes official reign. This is *impossible* if the 7th year of Artaxerxes was 459 BC to 458 BC. In fact, It can be seen that the 7th regnal year of Artaxerxes *must be* Tishri 1, 458 BC - Elul 29, 457 BC to satisfy all scriptural requirements. As shown previously, Ezra would have left Babylon on Nisan 1, 457 BC and arrived in Babylon 4 months later on Av 1, 457 BC. The decree must have been issued before he left no earlier than Tishri 1, 458 BC by Artaxerxes. These inescapable facts show that the 1st official year of Artaxerxes was not Tishri 1, 465 BC to Elul 29, 464 BC, but must be Tishri 1, 464 BC to Elul 29, 463 BC. In fact, this is the only year that will work using the Hebrew calendar or the Babylonian Calendar. Phillips has written two books which show beyond a reasonable doubt that Christ began his earthly ministry on *Tishri 15* which was the 1st day of the *Feast of Tabernacles*. This has also been shown true by Fred R. Coulter, *The Appointed Times of Jesus the Messiah* and *The Day That Jesus Christ Died*. See also Richard S. Thompson, http://www.hfbcbiblestudy.org/; Major Dan, https://www.historyandheadlines.com/april-7-30-ad-crucifixion-death-jesus-christ-think/; C. D. Franklin, and many others.

The Birth of Christ and the Daniel Prophecy

Phillips and others have proposed and presented convincing evidence to support a Nisan 14 (Wednesday, April 6) 30 AD crucifixion date for Jesus Christ. The year 30 AD falls in the middle of Daniel's 70th week, that is approximately 486.5 years since the 490 year prophecy started (Daniel 9: 26-27). Clearly, this leaves 3.5 years to finish the prophecy. Many modern prophecy teachers allow the 490 years to expire on Tishri 1 (Sept/Oct) of 33 AD. The event designated to end the prophecy is proposed to be the stoning of Stephen in Acts 6. Proponents of this theory (rightly so) identify this event as the final act of rejection of Jesus Christ as the promised Messiah by the Corporate Nation of Israel. From this point on, the message of salvation under the New Covenant passed to the Gentiles. We totally reject the logic which ends Daniel's 70th week in 33 AD based upon two platforms. ***First***, we have already discussed in some detail the things which must be completed before Daniel's 70 weeks of years expires, and several things can only be accomplished at the second advent of Jesus Christ. This reason is enough to reject the ***Steven hypothesis***. A ***second*** and more compelling reason is the stoning of Steven. In Acts 1-2 we are told how the Holy Spirit fell on the Feast of Pentecost, 50 days after the resurrection. Chapter 3 records a post-Pentecost miracle, the healing of a lame man, followed by Peter's sermon. Chapters 4:1 - 6:7 are concerned with the beginning of persecutions and the preparation for spreading the gospel. Acts 6: 8 records how Steven ***full of faith and power*** did ***great wonders and miracles***. The Jewish leaders turned against him, fearing that he would ***destroy this place, and change the customs***. At this point Stephen delivered perhaps the most powerful sermon ever preached (Acts 7: 1-53) . When he finished his discourse, the Jews cast him out of the city and stoned him. So, Steven became the first Christian to be martyred after the day of Pentecost. The conversion of Paul (Saul) is recorded in Acts 9. This must have been within a year after Christ was crucified. Saul had witnessed the crucifixion of Christ, and the stoning of Steven. He then received a letter from Rome to further persecute and kill any Jew who would follow after Christ. It is unlikely that the stoning of Steven took place 3.5 years after the crucifixion. The ***third*** and most important reason is that when Christ was crucified on Passover, Nisan 14 in 30 AD He cried out that ***It is finished***. The agony, torture and persecution on the Cross of Calvary was finished......The sin issue was finished....and the Old Covenant was finished. The *New Covenant* and the *Church Age* had begun. Less than 24 hours earlier at the Lord's Last Supper, He arose and passed a Cup of Wine around to all of His apostles. He clearly said:

This is my blood of the new testament, which is shed for many for the remission of sins Matthew 26:28

In the original Greek language this should read:

28 τοῦτο	γάρ	ἐστιν	τὸ	αἷμά	μου	,	τῆς	διαθήκης	,	τὸ	περὶ	πολλῶν
This	for	is	the	blood	of Me		of the	covenant		-	for	many

ἐκχυννόμενον	εἰς	ἄφεσιν	ἁμαρτιῶν	.
being poured out	for	forgiveness	of sins	

When Jesus Christ died on the Cross of Calvary He died for the forgiveness of all sins, and his sacrificial death initiated (by His own words) the ***New Covenant***. The Dispensation of the Law and the Old Covenant was finished and the New Covenant had begun. Note that up until this point in time that Jesus had gone to the Jews first, but now He would turn to the Gentiles. This and the Age of Grace was completely hidden and unknown to the Jews....It was a mystery revealed by the Apostle Paul. Salvation would now be by faith and grace, to both Jew and Gentiles alike. Please do not miss the implication of this truth. God had been dealing with the Jews ever since the Daniel prophecy began in 458 BC. He continued to deal exclusively with the Jews...not the Gentiles...until Christ was crucified on the Cross of Calvary. *Daniel is a Jewish prophecy*, and when God turned away from them and offered salvation to the Gentiles, the 70th week of Daniel would be interrupted until God would once again begin dealing with the Jews during the Tribulation Period which is the Time of Jacob's Trouble. *Alas! for that day is great, so that none is like it: it is even the **Time of Jacob's Trouble**; but he shall be saved out of it* (Jeremiah 30:7).

The entire church age was a *gap in time* which was not known before Paul revealed its mystery.

*For I would not, brethren, that ye should be ignorant of this **mystery**, lest ye should be wise in your own conceits; that blindness in part is happened to Israel, until the fullness of the Gentiles be come in* Romans 11:25

*This is a great **mystery**: but I speak concerning Christ and the church* Ephesians 5:32

When will God once more begin dealing with the corporate Jews? Most prophecy scholars agree that the 70th week of Daniel will be resumed when the *Great Tribulation* begins.

We have already thoroughly discussed the things that were to be accomplished by the end of Daniel's 70th week, and all of those things will not be *fully accomplished* until the end of the Age of Grace, or the Church age. Daniels last week (7 years) of the 70 week prophecy is not interrupted with 7 years remaining when He came to be baptized by John, but it would continue for another 3.5 years as Christ preached to the Jews...not to the Gentiles.

*These twelve Jesus sent forth, and commanded them, saying, **Go not into the way of the Gentiles**, and into any city of the Samaritans **enter ye n**ot* Matthew 10:12

This left 3.5 years yet to pass which will begin when God resumes his dealing with the nation of Israel. This will be the great tribulation period which will begin when Satan is cast down from heaven (Revelation 12:9), the Antichrist and false prophet arise (Revelation 13: 1-14), and the peace covenant is terminated with Israel (Isaiah 28: 15-18). This is when God will resume His efforts to heal and redeem Israel. As the tribulation period unfolds, it will last only 3.5 years; which is the last half of Daniel's 70th week of years (Revelation 12:14).

Why has this been so hard to believe? the earthly ministry of Christ as recorded in Matthew, Mark, Luke and John was to the JEWS...not the Gentiles. Once this is understood, it is inconceivable that these 3.5 years would not be contiguously contained within the initial part of Daniels 70 week prophecy to the Jews, and that the last 7 years of the Daniel prophecy must be interrupted as God turns to the gentiles. *Does this fit with the duration of the Great Tribulation?* Not only does it fit, but it makes perfect sense. The Wrath of Satan and the Wrath of God does not take place until after Satan is cast down to earth in Revelation 12. The Antichrist will not arise until Revelation 13. Satan is allowed to persecute all Jews and Gentiles for approximately 3.5 years.

It has always intrigued this author that the earthly ministry of Jesus Christ lasted 3.5 years, and that the period of time that Satan will attack and kill as many Christians as he can in the Great Tribulation is also 3.5 years in duration. This now makes perfect sense once it is realized that the 70 week prophecy of Daniel is dealing with a prophecy to the *Jews*, and no one else. The earthly ministry of Christ will begin 483 years after Nebuchadnezzar issued a decree to Ezra the scribe in 458 BC. Christ will be dealing with the Jews for another 3.5 years until He is crucified. There will then be a "gap in time" as God turns to the Gentiles and the Church Age begins to come to an end. The last week (7 years) of Daniels prophecy will resume once again when Satan begins His 3.5 year reign of terror against all Jews and Christians. Before these last 3.5 years of the Daniel prophecy begin, there will be tribulation as prophesied by Christ in Matthew 24. Christ Himself said that we are to be aware that this persecution is **not the end.**

[**7**] *For nation shall rise against nation, and kingdom against kingdom: and there shall be famines, and pestilences, and earthquakes, in divers places.*
[**8**] *All these are the **beginning of sorrows*** Matthew 24: 7-8

*Study to shew thyself approved unto God, a workman that need not to be ashamed, **rightly** dividing the word of truth* II Timothy 2:16

The last half of Daniels 70th week will now be examined in great detail.

Chapter 3

A Chronology and Timeline for The Great Tribulation

Traditional Interpretation

Prophecy students and pastors almost unanimously equate the time designations of 42 months and a time, times and half -a-time in the Book of Revelation with 1260 days. Where this interpretation actually came from is lost in the annals of history, but this universal interpretation seems to have little or no basis. *First*, there are 5 different references to these periods of time in the Book of Revelation and one in Daniel 12:7. At first glance, 42 months, time, times and half-a-time, and 1260 days all seem to refer to 3.5 years. However, 42 months is not 1260 days on almost any calendar. In fact, within any one yearly calendar, 42 months can be of a different duration depending upon where one starts and ends. The Hebrew phrase of time, times and half-a-time is universally equated to 3.5 years but *how long is 3.5 years in days*? It is both interesting and instructive that based upon the way God measures time in Genesis 1:14 a year is generally recognized as 365.2422 days and a lunar month as about 29.531 days. Based upon these well known durations, 42 months would be (42*29.531)=1242 days and 3.5 solar years would be (365.2422*3.5)=1278 days: neither are 1260 days. *Second*, individual references to a certain period of time refer to distinct events which do not usually start and end at the same point in the Revelation Period. *Third*, if the Jewish calendar is used to measure time in the Tribulation then there must be at least one leap year with an extra month of 29 days in some year. Nevertheless, we will first use a common duration of 1260 days for each time reference and see where this will take us. We will then investigate the case where these three measures of time are not all identical. Three observations will guide our investigation. *First*, regardless of how far back in antiquity the modern Hebrew calendar might have been used, the last 3.5 years of Daniel's week in the Book of Revelation have not yet taken place (Revelation 4:1, Revelation 1:1). *Second*, it is generally believed that the Great Tribulation might begin at almost any time, and when it does the Hebrew Calendar will be used by the Jews to mark days, weeks, months and years consistent with the first 486.5 years of the Daniel prophecy. *Third*, every event in the Book of Revelation has either a known start date, a known ending date, or both. A generic, common chronology of the last 3.5 years of the Tribulation is on the next page. The duration of the last 3.5 years of the tribulation is shown as 1267 days. This is determined by assuming that the 3.5 year ministry of Christ began at the River Jordan on the 1st day of the *Feast of Tabernacles* which is Tishri 15, 26 AD. His earthly ministry ended on the *Feast of Pentecost*, Nisan 14 in 30 AD. Using modern computer software it can be determined that ***the***

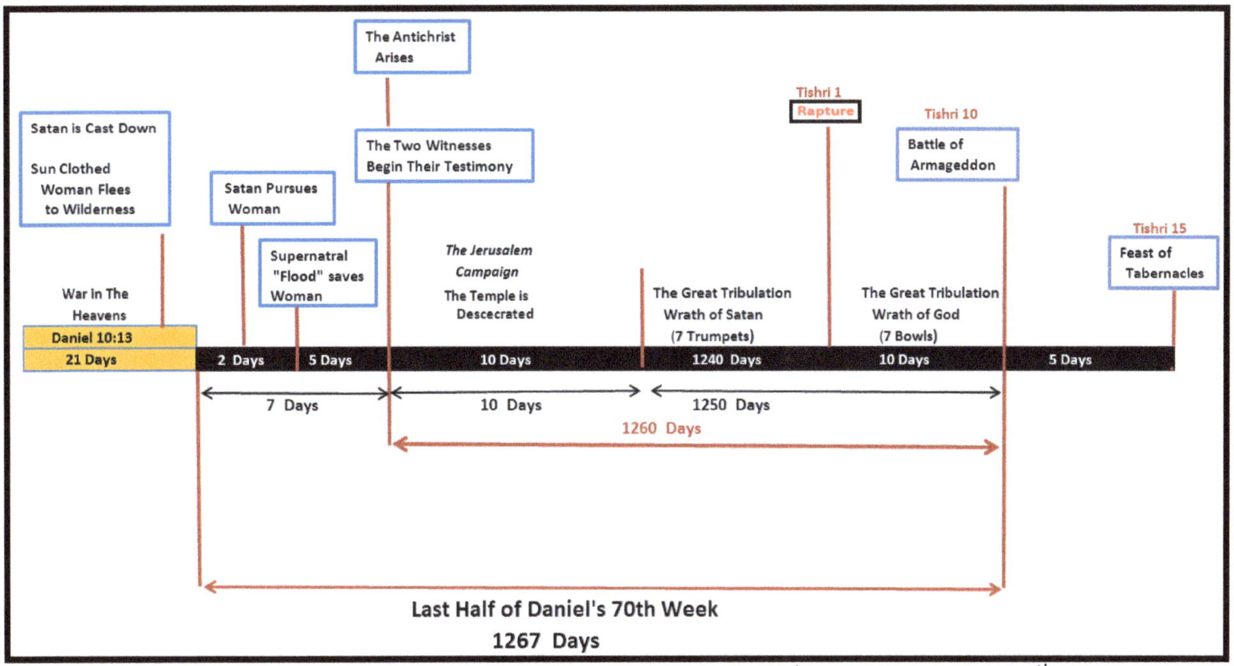

earthly ministry of Jesus Christ was 1297 days. This was the 1st part of Daniel's 70th week. The second half of Daniel's 70th week will resume when Satan is cast out of heaven and confined to this earth. We have no idea when this conflict might begin or end, but we do know that the Great Tribulation will end at the Battle of Armageddon on Tishri 10. It can be safely conjectured that the tribulation period will resume on a future Thursday, Nisan 15 (the 1st half ended at the Crucifixion of Jesus on Wednesday, Nisan 14). ***If*** the last 3.5 years ***began*** on Thursday, Nisan 15 in 30 AD and continued to when it would ***end*** on the *Feast of Yom Kippur* in 33 AD, this period of time would be **1267 days**: Therefore, the last half of Daniels 70th week will last ***1267 days***........not the generally assumed 1260 days. It is interesting that from the 7th and last day of the *Feast of Unleavened Bread* (Nisan 21) to the Battle of Armageddon (Tishri 10)...which will end the Tribulation Period.... is exactly 1260 days. We will return to this fact later.

Note also that Revelation 12 gives no duration for the great heavenly conflict between Michael and Satan. However, when Daniel was praying for wisdom and understanding in Daniel 10:13 he prayed for 21 days before Gabriel came to him. During this period of time, the angel Gabriel was intercepted by the *Prince of Persia* who tried to stop him. He might have succeeded if the Archangel Michael had not come to help him. The duration of the heavenly conflict is not important to this study, since the last half of Daniel's 70th week will not begin until the battle is finished and Satan is cast down to the earth. We will use 21 days just for display purposes.

The following table is a summary of when the 5 different events occur in the Book of Revelation; the biblical duration of each event, when each starts, when each ends, and the scriptural reference.

Time Period	Start	Finish	Scriptural Reference
42 Months	From When the Beast (Antichrist) Arises	Antichrist is Destroyed at The Battle of Armageddon	Revelation 13:5
42 Months	The Rebuilt Temple will be taken over by Antichrist	The Jewish Temple will be tread Underfoot by Gentiles for 42 Months	Revelation 11:2
1260 Days	Two Witnesses will Start Prophesying	They will prophesy until the Saints (Jews and Gentiles) are Raptured. They will then be killed and lay in street 3.5 days. God will then say: "Come up Here"	Revelation 11:3
1260 Days	Woman is Nourised In wilderness	Until Jesus Comes for Them After Battle of Armageddon	Revelation 12:6
Time, Times and Half a Time	The Woman (Israel) of Revelation 12 is nourished in the wilderness from the dragon (Satan)	The Jews in the wilderness will be nourished to keep them alive so that they can enter the Millennial Kingdom and inherit the Promised land	Revelation 12:14

Each of these 5 events will now be placed on the common, generic chronology shown on the Previous page. Each of the five different time-related events will be color coded for easy reference. ***42 months and time,times and half-a-time will all be assumed to last 1260 days.***

The Reign of Antichrist

Time Period	Start	Finish	Scriptural Reference
42 Months 1242 days	From When the Beast (Antichrist) Arises	Antichrist is Destroyed at The Battle of Armageddon	Revelation 13:5

[1] *And I stood upon the sand of the sea, and saw a beast rise up out of the sea, having seven heads and ten horns, and upon his horns ten crowns, and upon his heads the name of blasphemy.*

[2] *And the beast which I saw was like unto a leopard, and his feet were as the feet of a bear, and his mouth as the mouth of a lion: and the dragon gave him his power, and his seat, and great authority.*

[3] *And I saw one of his heads as it were wounded to death; and his deadly wound was healed: and all the world wondered after the beast.*

[4] *And they worshipped the dragon which gave power unto the beast: and they worshipped the beast, saying, Who is like unto the beast? who is able to make war with him?*

[**5**] *And there was given unto him a mouth speaking great things and blasphemies; and power was given unto him to continue* ***forty and two months.*** Revelation 13: 1-5

Satan is identified as the *dragon* in Revelation 13:9. The *beast* is how John describes the *Antichrist*. He arises up out of the *sea* which represents the sea of *humanity*. He is that great world leader who will unify Europe under a 7 Nation confederacy. When he arises, he will come up among 10 European nations...each of which were once a part of the old Roman empire. He will attack and conquer 3 of these nations, and the other 7 will capitulate to his great authority and military might (Daniel 7). This is evident because when he appears in Revelation 13:1 he has 10 crowns and 7 horns upon his head.....he is the soverign ruler over all of the of original 10 nations (He wears 10 crowns on 10 horns), and he has 7 horns, which means he has conquered 3 nations. John describes him in evil glory....He is quick as a leopard, strong as a bear, mighty as a lion (Daniel 13:2) and he (the Antichrist) has been given great power by the dragon (Satan, Revelation 13:4). Satan has taken over his body and mind, *but how*? He will evidently be *wounded unto death* by a sword or a knife (Revelation 13:3, Revelation 13:12, Revelation 13:14). God permits Satan to revive this great world leader from death, and Satan then completely takes control of his mind and actions. ***This revived individual is who we call the Antichrist***. Satan is a spiritual, angelic creature and he needs a body. Satan will then energize a 2nd evil man called the *False Prophet* (Revelation 13: 11-14). Their first act will be to attack Jerusalem in the *Armageddon Campaign* (Phillips; The Book of Revelation).

They will immediately overun the City and enter the temple....where the Antichrist will sit upon a throne and demand to be worshipped as God (Daniel 11:31, Matthew 24: 15-16). Power is granted to the Antichrist to conduct a reign of terror for 42 months (Revelaion 11:2), which we

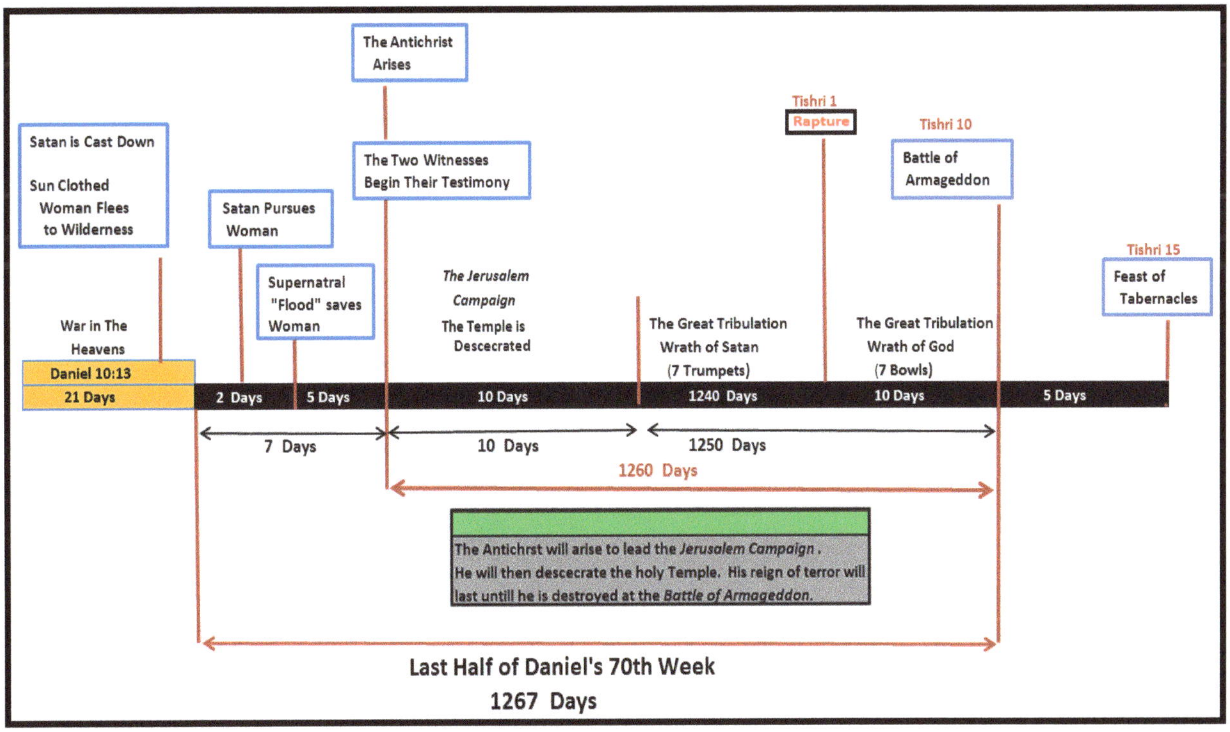

assume is 1260 days until Christ destroys him at the *Battle of Armageddon*. The 1st seven days will be explained later.

The Rebuilt Temple Will Be Descecrated

Time Period	Start	Finish	Scriptural Reference
42 Months	The Rebuilt Temple will be taken over by Antichrist	The Jewish Temple will be tread Underfoot by Gentiles for 42 Months	Revelation 11:2

[**1**] *And there was given me a reed like unto a rod: and the angel stood, saying, Rise, and measure the temple of God, and the altar, and them that worship therein.*
[**2**] *But the court which is without the temple leave out, and measure it not; for it is given unto the Gentiles: and the holy city shall they tread under foot* ***forty and two months*** Rev. 11: 1-2

In Revelation 11: 1-2 John is approached by *an angel* who gives him a *reed* which is a measuring stick that resembles a *rod*. John is told to go and measure the *Temple and the Alter* therein, but do not measure the *outer court* because it is given over to the Gentiles. The context of this command is to understand that the gentiles who are in view here are the ungodly followers of Satan and anyone who has not accepted Christ. The *holy city* is almost certainly the earthly City of Jerusalem. It is not uncommon to hear prophecy teachers claim that the Holy Temple that was destroyed by Rome in 70 AD would never be rebuilt. Revelation 11: 1-2 completely destroys this concept. Before the last 3.5 years of Great Tribulation (1267 days) can take place the Jerusalem Temple will be rebuilt. The Jews will also resume temple worship and sacrifices as a part of Israel's *Covenant with Death*. This will all cease when the Satanically indwelled Antichrist will enter the temple and declare himself as God.

And all that dwell upon the earth shall worship ***him*** (the antichrist), (those)*whose names are not written in the Book of Life of the Lamb, slain from the foundation of the world* Revelation 13:8

John is told to go and measure the *Temple and the Alter* therein, but do not measure the *outer court* because it is given over to the Gentiles. The context of this command is to understand that the gentiles who are in view here were in Old Testament times considered to be heathens who could enter the temple no further than the outer court. The *holy city* is almost certainly the earthly City of Jerusalem. It is not uncommon to hear prophecy teachers claim that the Holy Temple that was destroyed by Rome in 70 AD would never be rebuilt. Revelation 11: 1-2 completely destroys this concept. Before the last 3.5 years of Great Tribulation can take place the Jerusalem Temple will be rebuilt. The Jews will also resume temple worship and sacrifices

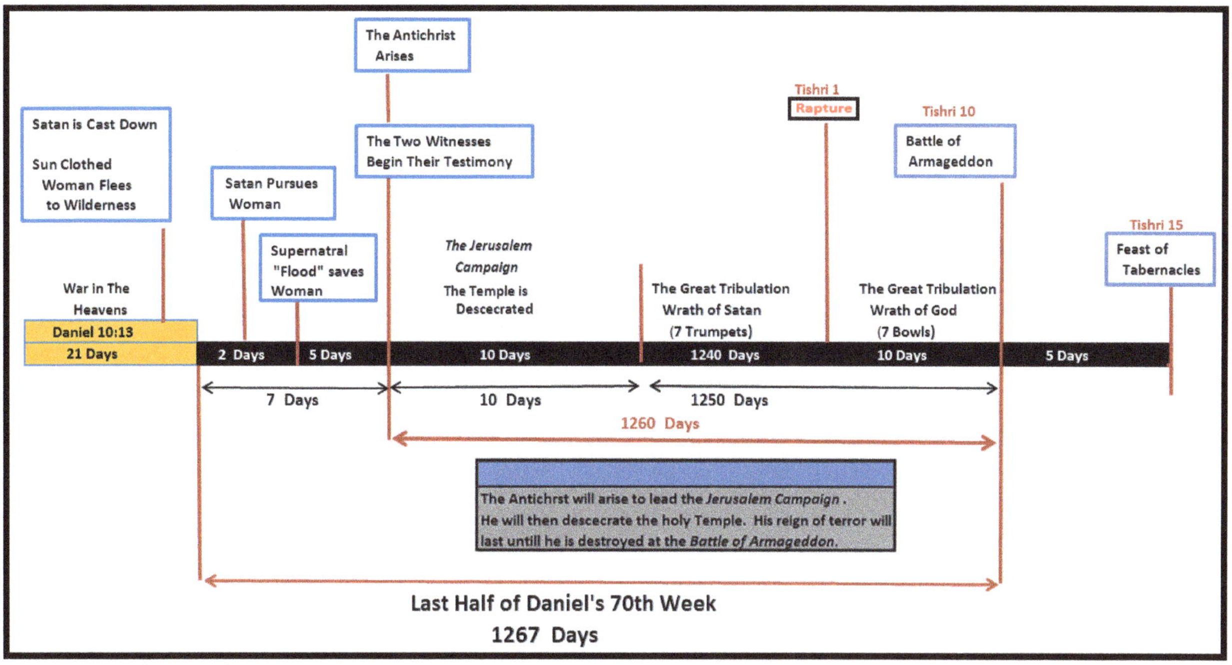

as a part of Satan's *Covenant with Death*. This will all cease when the Satanically indwelled Antichrist will enter the temple and declare himself as God.

Two Witnesses Will Prophesy For 1260 Days

In the face of this apostasy, two witnesses for Jesus Christ will stand in or near the temple and declare the eternal gospel.

1260 Days	Two Witnesses will Start Prophesying	They will prophesy until the Saints (Jews and Gentiles) are Raptured. They will then be killed and lay in street 3.5 days. God will then say: "Come up Here"	Revelation 11:3

[3] *And I will give power unto my two witnesses, and they shall prophesy a* ***thousand two hundred and threescore days****, clothed in sackcloth.*
[4] *These are the two olive trees, and the two candlesticks standing before the God of the earth.*
[5] *And if any man will hurt them, fire proceedeth out of their mouth, and devours their enemies: and if any man will hurt them, he must in this manner be killed.*
[6] *These have power to shut heaven, that it rain not in the days of their prophecy: and have power over waters to turn them to blood, and to smite the earth with all plagues, as often as they will.*
[7] *And when they shall have finished their testimony, the beast that ascends out of the bottomless pit shall make war against them, and shall overcome them, and kill them.*
[8] And their dead bodies shall lie in the street of the great city, which spiritually is called Sodom and Egypt, where also our Lord was crucified.

[**9**] *And they of the people and kindreds and tongues and nations shall see their dead bodies three days and an half, and shall not suffer their dead bodies to be put in graves.*
[**10**] *And they that dwell upon the earth shall rejoice over them, and make merry, and shall send gifts one to another; because these two prophets tormented them that dwelt on the earth.*
[**11**] *And after three days and an half the Spirit of life from God entered into them, and they stood upon their feet; and great fear fell upon them which saw them.*
[**12**] *And they heard a great voice from heaven saying unto them, Come up hither. And they ascended up to heaven in a cloud; and their enemies beheld them* Revelation 11: 3-12

When the Antichrist will arise and demand that He be worshipped as God, two witnesses will be divinely appointed by God to tell all Jews and true believers to hold fast.... face tribulation....and do not be afraid because those who do not capitulate to the demands of the Antichrist may be martyred, but they will inherit eternal life if they are faithful.

The two witnesses will be annointed and preach for 1260 days. They will be clothed in *sackcloth* and receive *great power*. Their message will be: *Do not worship the beast*, no matter what the consequences might be of *not* doing so. There are two specific warnings: (1) Do not take the *mark of the beast* and (2) Do not worship the *graven image* of the Antichrist.

The antichhrist will demand that all who live upon the earth will worship him and him alone. The antichrist is neither omnipotent or omnicient; he cannot be all over the world and threaten people everywhere to capitulate or die. *How can this possibly come to pass?* Immediately folowing the arise of the antichrist, Satan will supernaturally initiate another evil person which we call the *False Prophet*. The false prophet will be appointed the world leader of a universal "church" which will worship Satan. He will imitate Christ and appear as a *Lamb*, but he speaks as a *dragon*.

[**11**] *And I beheld another beast coming up out of the earth; and he had two horns like a lamb, and he spoke as a dragon.*
[**12**] *And he exercises all the power of the first beast before him, and causes the earth and them which dwell therein to worship the first beast, whose deadly wound was healed.*
[**13**] *And he doeth great wonders, so that he maketh fire come down from heaven on the earth in the sight of men,*
[**14**] *And deceives them that dwell on the earth by the means of those miracles which he had power to do in the sight of the beast; saying to them that dwell on the earth, that* ***they should make an image to the beast, which had the wound by a sword, and did live****.*
[**15**] *And he had power to give life unto the image of the beast, that the image of the beast should both speak, and cause that as many as would not worship the image of the beast should be killed* Revelation 13: 11-15

At this point, the scriptures reveal a fact that is seldom if ever taught by any prophecy teacher. It is with great sorrow that the following truth is now fully revealed. The *False Prophet* has been given great power by Satan (Revelation 13: 12). He causes fire to come down from the sky and performs miracles (Revelation 13: 13-14). The most deadly power that he possesses is that he will make an image of the beast (antichrist) and incredibly it will come to life.....it will actually speak and command all in the sound of the image's voice to worship the antichist or *die* (Revelation 13:15). There will be millions of these images created by the False Prophet and distributed all over the world. This is how the antichrist will demand to be worshipped by all who live in Israel, other countries and other continents (Revelation 12:17). It is no wonder that Christ declared: *And except those days should be shortened, there should no flesh be saved: but for the elect's sake those days shall be shortened* (Matthew 24:22). *How will those days be shortened*? The elect will be raptured out, but *not before* the Tribulation begins. *How could days be shortened if the elect never had to endure any of them?* The elect will be raptured out as the 7th trumpet sounds. The *shortened days* are the 10 days of God's Wrath between the *Feast of Trumpets* (Rapture) and the *Feast of Yom Kippur* (Battle of Armageddon). These are the days during which the *Wrath of God is poured out upon the desolate*. This is called a *Pre-Wrath* rapture. It is fully developed by Phillips; The Book of Revelation: *Mysteries Revealed*. Those who may be skeptical and have been indoctrinated into what is called a *Pre-Tribulation Rapture* should read Revelation 11: 15-18, Revelation 12:17 and Revelation 15: 1-8 with no preconceived bias. Those who choose to follow after Satan will be *marked* in their *right hand* or in their *foreheads*. It is commonly assumed that this mark is the number 666 (Revelation 13: 16-18). Those who do not display this mark will not be allowed to buy or sell anything.

[**16**] *And he causes all, both small and great, rich and poor, free and bond, to receive a mark in their right hand, or in their foreheads:*
[**17**] *And that no man might buy or sell, save he that had the mark, or the name of the beast, or the number of his name* Revelation 13: 6-7

There are irreversable eternal consequences for those who take the mark of the beast.

And the beast was taken, and with him the false prophet that wrought miracles before him, with which he deceived them that ***had received the mark of the beast, and them that worshipped his image****. These both were cast alive into a lake of fire burning with brimstone* Revelation 19:20

For those who refuse to worship Satan and refuse the mark, there are great rewards.

And I saw thrones, and they sat upon them, and judgment was given unto them: and I saw the souls of them that were beheaded for the witness of Jesus, and for the word of God, and which had not worshipped the beast, neither his image, neither had received his mark upon their foreheads, or in their hands; and they lived and reigned with Christ a thousand years Revelation 20:4

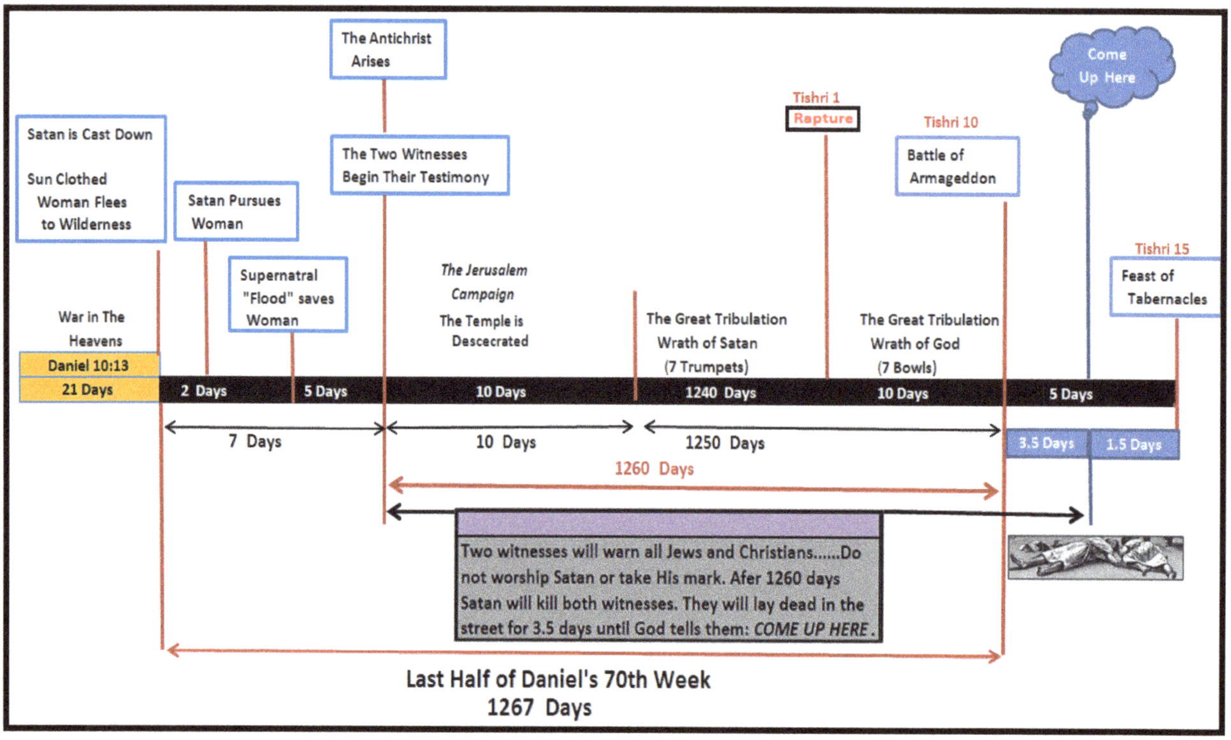

The Woman is Fed In A Place Prepared by God for 1260 Days

Time Period	Start	Finish	Scrriptural Reference
1260 Days	Woman is Fed in A Place Prepared by God	Until Jesus Comes For Them After Battle of Armageddon	Revelation 12:6

And the woman fled into the wilderness, where she hath a place prepared of God, that they should feed her there a thousand two hundred and threescore days Revelation 12:6

The *woman* has previously been identified as *Israel* who is the mother of us all (Galatians 4:26). The apostle Paul revealed: *Know ye therefore that they which are of faith, the same are the children of Abraham* (Galatians 3:7). Those who fled into the wilderness are often identified as only the Jews, but this is unlikely since when God supernaturally protected the *woman* Satan turned to persecute the *remnant of her seed which keep the commandments of God, and have the testimony of Jesus Christ*. There is no distinction between Jews and Gentiles in the New Covenant. It is also possible that a remnant of her seed is the 144,000 (12,000 from 12 tribes of Israel) who have previously been sealed against Tribulation Wrath. However, this is also not likely. *Why would these 144,000 be sealed if they are going to be protected in the wilderness*? It is suggested that these 144,000 have been sealed for two reasons: (1) Protect them as they witness for Christ to their fellow Jews during the last half of Daniel's 70th week (2) Protect them so that they can form the core of those redeemed Jews who will live in the promised land during the Millennial Kingdom (Phillips; The Millennial Kingdom: *Life After the Great Tribulation*).

...the dragon was wroth with the woman, and went to make war with the remnant of her seed, which keep the commandments of God, and have the testimony of Jesus Christ Rev. 12:17

The starting point of this protection is when this remnant flees from the City of Jerusalem before and during the *Jerusalem Campaign*. Christ warned the Jewish people to flee quickly when the Temple is desecrated by the antichrist in His *Olivet Discourse* (Matthew 24: 15-21). This group will need to be protected until Satan, the Antichrist and the False Prophet are all captured and condemned by Christ at the Battle of Armageddon.

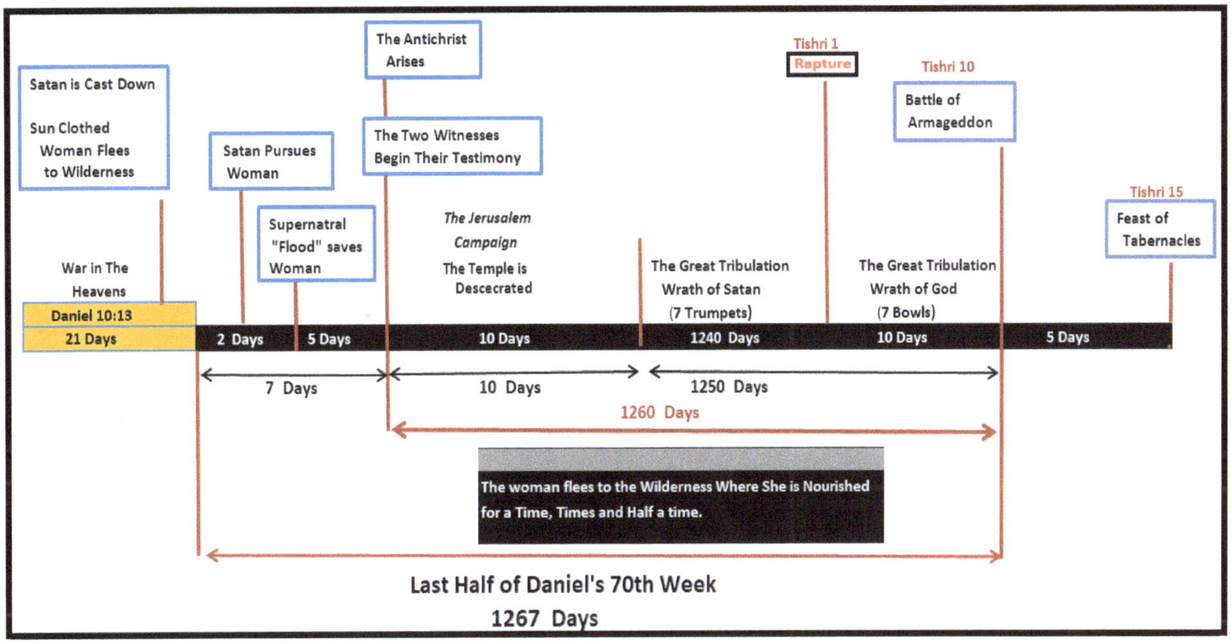

The Woman is Nourished in the Wilderness for a Time, Times and Half-a-Time

Time Period	Start	Finish	Scriptural Reference
Time, Times and Half a Time 1267 Days	The Woman (Israel) of Revelation 12 is nourished in the wilderness from the dragon (Satan)	The Jews in the wilderness will be nourished to keep them alive so that they can enter the Millennial Kingdom and inherit the Promised land	Revelation 12:14

[13] *And when the dragon saw that he was cast unto the earth, he persecuted the woman which brought forth the man child.*
[14] *And to the woman were given two wings of a great eagle, that she might fly into the wilderness, into her place, where she is nourished for a* ***time, and times, and half a time****, from the face of the serpent*
[15] *And the serpent cast out of his mouth water as a flood after the woman, that he might cause her to be carried away of the flood.*
[16] *And the earth helped the woman, and the earth opened her mouth, and swallowed up the flood which the dragon cast out of his mouth.*
[17] *And the dragon was wroth with the woman, and went to make war with the remnant of her seed, which keep the commandments of God, and have the testimony of Jesus Christ.*
Revelation 12: 13-17

And to the woman were given two wings of a great eagle, that she might fly into the wilderness, into her place, where she is nourished for a time, and times, and half a time, from the face of the serpent Revelation 12:14

How is this woman nourished? It is not clear how the woman is nourished, but two possibilities can be postulated. *First*, God is quite capable of feeding and protecting those who He chooses. The Children of Israel were nourished by manna and quail for 40 years in the wilderness. Elijah was fed by raven after he fled in fear from Jezebel, and King David was nourished when He hid from Saul in a remote cave. The *Second* possibility is that this remnant fled to a special place in the wilderness where they will be fed and protected by those who lived there. Many have proposed that they fled to the city of *Petra*. Those who would protect and nourish this remnant might be a part of the Sheep in the *Judgment of the Sheep and Goats* following the Battle of Armageddon. The term *wings of eagles* does not mean by helicopter or plane as some have assumed. This simply implies the woman will flee quickly, and their strength will come from God. Wings of Eagles is found twice in the holy scriptures.

Ye have seen what I did unto the Egyptians, and how I bare you on eagles' wings, and brought you unto myself Exodus 19:4

But they that wait upon the LORD shall renew their strength; they shall mount up with wings as eagles; they shall run, and not be weary; and they shall walk, and not faint Isaiah 40:31

The woman which will *fly into the wilderness* (not literally, but quickly) is assumed by all prophecy teachers as the same woman seen in Revelation 12:6, and they will be protected and nourished a time, time and half a time which is assumed to be 1260 days. In Revelation 12: 15-16 additional information is revealed concerning how the fleeing remant is saved from the pursuing Satan. The old serpent (Satan/the Dragon) evidently attempts to destroy all who are fleeing from Jerusalem with a great flood of water (Revelation 12:15). Satan obviousy intends to drown those fleeing just as the army of the Pharogh was destroyed by water at the Exodus in the Red Sea. However, God will save His people (again) by supernatural means. The earth will *open* and *swallow up the flood.* Satan is absolutely furious.....He has been cast out of heaven and confined to this earth, the Man-Child has escaped him, and now those who flee from him have been supernaturally saved. He is *wroth with the woman*. In the Greek the word wroth is *orge* and it literally means to be *furious or extremely angry*. There are two Greek words which ar used in this context.....*orge* and *thumas*. Thumas is a deep anger which is controlled. Orge is like a teapot which explodes. Satan is furious, and he now turns upon a remnant of her seed: *the remnant of her seed which keep the commandments of God, and have the testimony of Jesus Christ* (Revelation 12:17). Notice that this completely destroys a Mid-Tribulation rapture theory.

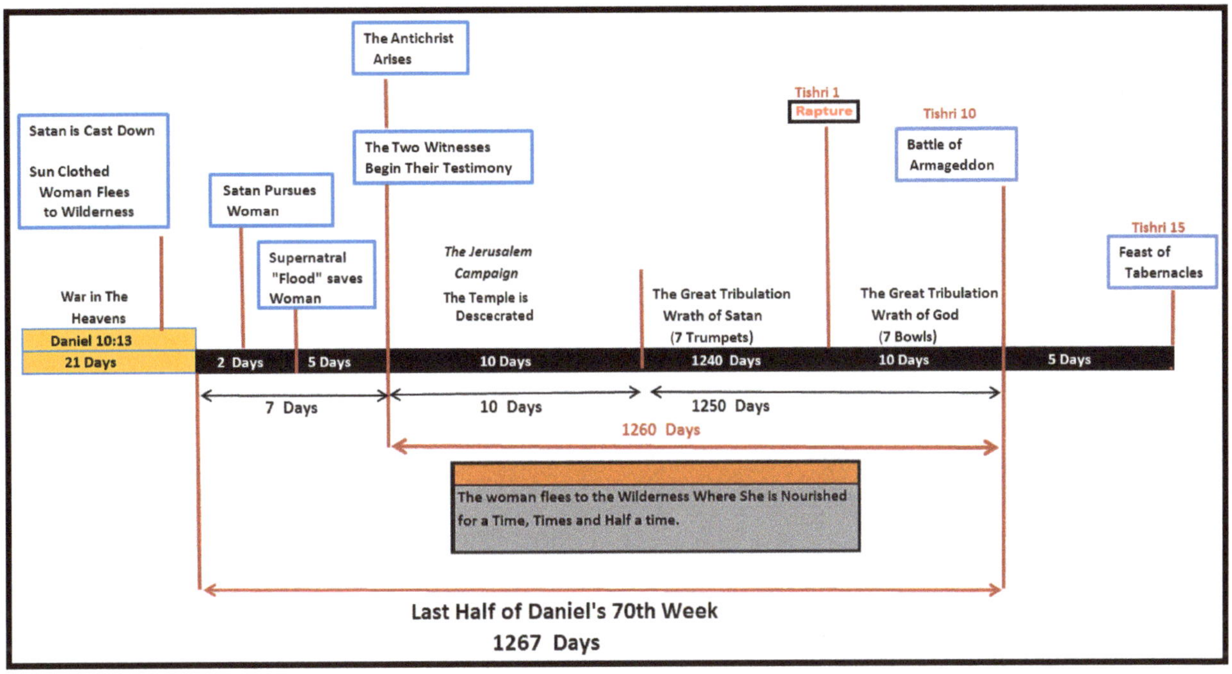

A New Interpretation

The previous analysis of the 5 different events revealed in the Book of Revelation has followed the traditional and widespread belief that each of the three different time periods of 1260 days, 42 months and time, times and half a time can all be equated to 3.5 years, and that 3.5 years is (42 months*30 days/Mo.) = 1260 days. However, we have shown that this is a questionable assumption and have also calculated that the last half of Daniel's 70th week is actually 1267 days. There are several reasons why this assumption might be challnged, but none is more important than the scriptual words themselves. At the core of this issue is: *If each time period is in fact 1260 days long or 3.5 years; Why would Christ use three different periods of time in less that two chapters without some good reason*?   If they were all of the same duration; *Then* *why would Jesus not use one measure of time?* This is illustrated forcefully by Revelation 12:6 and Revelation 12:14.

And the woman fled into the wilderness, where she hath a place prepared of God, that they should feed her there a ***thousand two hundred and threescore days*** Revelation 12:6

And to the woman were given two wings of a great eagle, that she might fly into the wilderness, into her place, where she is nourished for a ***time, and times, and half a time*** Revelation 12:14

Within the short space of only 8 verses, Jesus used two different measures of time. This defies all logic and consistency of record if they are both 1260 days long. Perhaps this has always been believed and accepted because there was never any way to determine the difference. Daniel said: *But thou, O Daniel, shut up the words, and seal the book, even to the time of the end: many shall run to and fro, and knowledge shall be increased* (Daniel 12:40). Knowledge today is being generated at an unprecedented rate. Use of the Jewish calendar to determine the length of days, weeks, months and years for any year in the future could never be accomplished without the impact and advancement of modern astronomy, NASA, brilliant computer programmers and modern digital computers. We have already determined that the Great Tribulation will be 1267 days in duration. The following investigation will be based upon several key assumptions. If any are found inaccurate or need to be changed, the following *approach* will still be valid.

Assumption 1: The Daniel prophecy began in September of 458 BC and was issued by the Babylonian King Artaxeres in his 7th year of reign.

Assumption 2: The 490 year Daniel Prophecy is based upon a year to a day principle. No one doubts that this is true.

Assumption 3: Each year is a Solar year of 365.2422 days as designed by God in Genesis 1:14

Assumption 4: Christ came to the River Jordan to be baptized by John the Baptizer in the Fall of 26 AD (This must be true by Assumptions 1-3)

Assumption 5: Christ came to the River Jordan to be baptized on Tishri 15 which was the 1st day of the Feast of Tabernacles.

Assumption 6: The ministry of Christ lasted approximately 3.5 years on the Hebrew Calendar from Tishri 15, 26 AD (Feast of Tabernacles) to Nisan 14, 30 AD (Feast of Pentecost)

Assumption 7: Christ was crucified on Wednesday, Nisan 14 in 30 AD. Many biblical scholars have proposed and justified this same date

Assumption 8: The personal pronoun *he* in Daniel 9:27 is not the Antichrist but is Jesus Christ. The Daniel Prophecy pertains to the Jews and how God will re-establish His covenant relationship with His chosen people...the Jews.

Assumption 9: When Christ was crucified, a "Gap in time" started that would continue until the Great Tribulation would start

Assumption 10: The first half of Daniel's 70th week was completed in the 3.5 years ministry of Christ.

Assumption 11: The last half of Daniel's 70th week will start when Satan is cast out of heaven and will end when Satan is defeated at the Battle of Armageddon.

Assumption 12: The last 3.5 years of the 70th week of Daniel is a time of great sorrow and persecution. It is called the *Time of Jacobs Trouble* and will last 1267 days.

These 12 assumptions are not arbitrary or unsubstantiated. They are all consistent with the biblical records in the Old Testament, the Book of Daniel and the Book of Revelation. Each are more fully justified and explained in Phillips; The Book of Revelation: *Mysteries Revealed* (606 Pages) and in Phillips; The Millennial Kingdom: *Life After The Great Tribulation* (146 Pages). The following generic diagram will be used as a template in the following presentations.

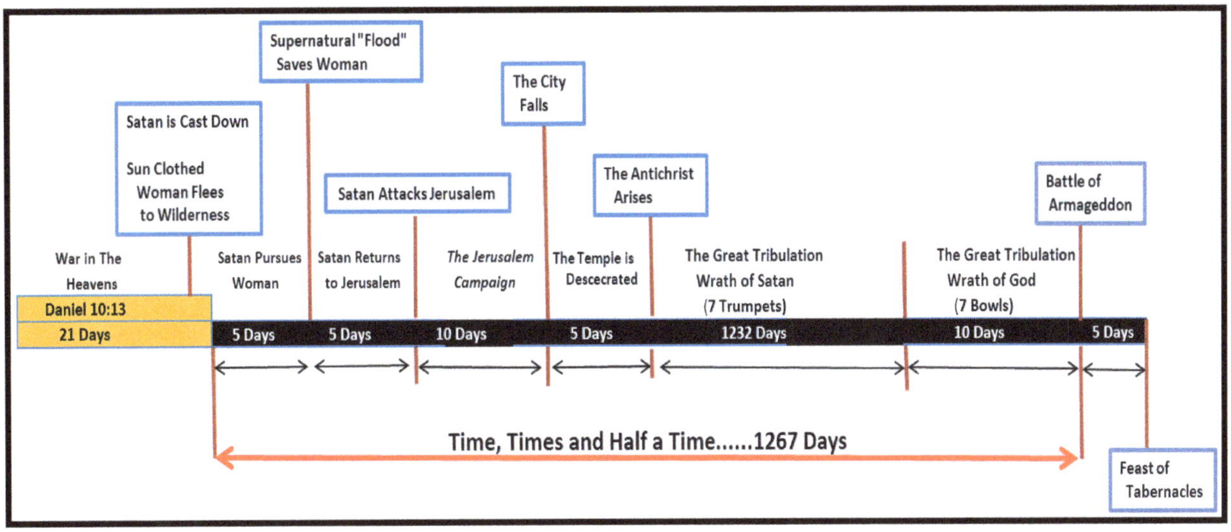

This last 3.5 years of Daniels 70th week will bring the *Wrath of Satan* (The 7 trumpet judgments) and the *Wrath of God* (The 7 Bowl/Vial judgments). It has already been determined that from the time that Satan is cast out of heaven until he is destroyed at the Battle of Armageddon is 1267 days. The Chronology of key end-time events is the same as before, but the time scale has changed slightly to realistically fit the duration of each event.

The 5 different periods of time and the associated events are shown on the next page. There are two different periods of time which must be determined: (1) 42 months and (2) Time, times and half-a-time. Of course, 1260 days are 1260 days. 42 months might be (42*29.53) = 1240 days or it might be (365.2422/12)*42 = 1278.5 days. The latter calculation can be rejected because it is longer that 1267 days, and some Hebrew years contain 13 months (Leap Years). A time,times and half-a-time is usually taken as identical to 3.5 years. This might be (365.2422*3.5) = 1278 days but this is also too long, and as we have previously discussed a period of 3.5 years is not specific. The duration of a time, times and half-a-time is best determined by context as we will see. The table on the next page illustrates the biblically designated time for each event in the Book of Revelation. This analysis will not assume that every time period is 1260 days, but the duration of each event will be determined from scriptural clues and context. The description of each major event has not changed to any great degree. With only minor changes each will be given again here to avoid looking back at the previous analysis. It has already been determined that the last half of Daniels 70th week is 1267 days induration. All events must by necessity fall within this time frame.

Time Period	Start	Finish	Scriptural Reference
42 Months	From When the Beast (Antichrist) Arises	Antichrist is Destroyed at The Battle of Armageddon	Revelation 13:5
42 Months	The Rebuilt Temple will be taken over by Antichrist	The Jewish Temple will be tread Underfoot by Gentiles for 42 Months	Revelation 11:2
1260 Days	Two Witnesses will Start Prophesying	They will prophesy until the Saints (Jews and Gentiles) are Raptured. They will then be killed and lay in street 3.5 days. God will then say: "Come up Here"	Revelation 11:3
1260 Days	Woman is Nourised In wilderness	Until Jesus Comes for Them After Battle of Armageddon	Revelation 12:6
Time, Times and Half a Time	The Woman (Israel) of Revelation 12 is nourished in the wilderness from the dragon (Satan)	The Jews in the wilderness will be nourished to keep them alive so that they can enter the Millennial Kingdom and inherit the Promised land	Revelation 12:14

The time duration for each of these events can be determined with reasonable accuracy by using the current Hebrew calendar, which will be in use when the Great Tribulation will start and end. The generic timeline previously shown cannot be completely determined from the scriptural records. The times shown are proposed and reasonable from the Book of Revelation and Jewish tradition. For example, it is certain that there are 10 days between the *Feast of Trumpets* (Tishri 1) and the *Feast of Yom Kippur* (Tishri 10). Many biblical prophecy teachers have proposed that the *Battle of Armageddon* will take place on Nisan 10. The timeline also shows that 5 days will pass between when the temple is descecrated and when the antichrist arises. This is not known for certain and is only an educated guess, but it cannot be far from the truth. This analysis assumes that the rapture will take place when the 7th trumpet sounds, and it is assumed that the *Wrath of God* will not fall upon believers (Revelation 14:19, Revelation 15:1), but only on unbelievers (Matthew 3:7, Romans 1:18, Romans 5:9, Ephesians 5:6, Collossians 3:6, I Thesselonians 1:10, I Thesselonians 5:9). These scriptures form the backbone of what is called a *Pre-Wrath Rapture Theology*. A pre-wrath rapture position is based upon the promise(s) that anyone who has accepted Christ as their Lord and savior will be spared from the Wrath of God....but no Christian has ever been promised that they would not suffer Tribulation

(John 16:33, Acts 14:22, Revelation 7:14). Can we determine from the holy scriptures what is the *Wrath of God*?.....***Yes.***

And I saw another sign in heaven, great and marvelous, seven angels having the seven last plagues; for in them is filled up the wrath of God Revelation 15:1

And I heard a great voice out of the temple saying to the seven angels, Go your ways, and pour out the vials of the wrath of God upon the earth Revelation 16:1

The Wrath of God is clearly stated twice to be the 7 Bowl/Vial judgments. The 7 Bowl/Vial judgments are immediately preceded by the sounding of the 7th trumpet. There has been much said about what must take place when the 7th trumpet sounds.

[**15**] *And the seventh angel sounded; and there were great voices in heaven, saying, The kingdoms of this world are become the kingdoms of our Lord, and of his Christ; and he shall reign forever and ever.*
[**18**] *And the nations were angry, and* ***thy wrath is come****, and the* ***time of the dead****, that* ***they should be judged****, and that* ***thou shouldest give reward unto thy servants the prophets, and to the saints, and them that fear thy name****, small and great; and shouldest* ***destroy them which destroy the earth*** Revelation 11: 15,18

In examining what will happen when the 7th trumpet sounds, it is difficult to not believe that this is the long awaited rapture and resurrection of all true believers. Carefully read the above promises, and if read with no preconcieved bias as to when the rapture has been taught by evangilists and preachers to occur, what are you persuaded to believe? The teaching of man or the truth of God? This entire line of reasoning is fully developed and justified in Phillips; The Book of Revelation: *Mysteries Revealed*.

The Reign of Antichrist

Time Period	Start	Finish	Scriptural Reference
42 Months	From When the Beast (Antichrist) Arises	Antichrist is Destroyed at The Battle of Armageddon	Revelation 13:5

[**1**] *And I stood upon the sand of the sea, and saw a beast rise up out of the sea, having seven heads and ten horns, and upon his horns ten crowns, and upon his heads the name of blasphemy.*
[**2**] *And the beast which I saw was like unto a leopard, and his feet were as the feet of a bear, and his mouth as the mouth of a lion: and the dragon gave him his power, and his seat, and great authority.*

[3] *And I saw one of his heads as it were wounded to death; and his deadly wound was healed: and all the world wondered after the beast.*
[4] *And they worshipped the dragon which gave power unto the beast: and they worshipped the beast, saying, Who is like unto the beast? who is able to make war with him?*
[5] *And there was given unto him a mouth speaking great things and blasphemies; and power was given unto him to continue* ***forty and two months.*** Revelation 13: 1-5

Satan is identified as the *dragon* in Revelation 13:9. The *beast* is how John describes the *Antichrist* (revelation 13:1). He arises up out of the *sea* which represents the sea of *humanity*. He is prefigured as that great world leader who will unify Europe under a 7 Nation confederacy. When he arises, he will come up among 10 European nations...each of which were once a member of the old Roman empire. He will attack and conquer 3 of these nations, and then all will capitulate to his great authority and military might. This is evident because he has 10 crowns upon his head.....He will be the ruler over all of the of original 10 nations (He wears 10 crowns on 10 horns), which he will unify into a 7 nation confederacy (he has 7 horns).....Daniel 7:23-24. John describes him in unprcedented but evil glory....He is quick as a leopard, strong as a bear, mighty as a lion and he has been given great power by the dragon (Satan). Satan has taken over his body and mind, but how? He had evidently been *wounded unto death* by a sword or a knife just after Satan turns on Jerusalem and breaks the *Peace Covenant* (Revelation 13:3, Revelation 13:12, Revelation 13:14). God permits Satan to revive this great world leader from death, and Satan then completely takes control of his mind and body. Satan is a spiritual, angelic creature and he needs a body from which to operate. Satan will then energize a 2nd evil man called the false prophet (Revelation 13: 11-14). Their first act will be to attack Jerusalem in what has been called the *Armageddon Campaign* (Phillips; The Book of Revelation: *Mysteries Revealed*). They will immediately overun the City and enter the temple....where the Antichrist will sit upon a throne and demand to be worshipped as God. Power will be granted to the Antichrist to conduct a reign of terror for 42 months (Revelation 11:2). We have already indicated that 42 months might be either 1240 or 1278.5 days. A more accurate estimate of how many days are in these 42 month is to realize that the end of the antichrist will be at the Battle of Armageddon on Tishri 10, The Feast of Yom Kippur. The future year on which this battle will take place is unknown, but it will be on the last day of the last half of Daniels 70th week. A *gap* in Daniels 70th week started on Nisan 15 in 30 AD, but if there had been no interuption of these last 7 years, then the 70th week would have ended on Tishri 10 in 33 AD. Working backward from Tishri 10 exactly 42 months, one can verify the Antichrist will arise on ***Monday, Iyyar 10*** (there is one extra month added during this

Nisan						
S	M	T	W	T	F	S
				1	2	3
4	5	6	7	8	9	10
11	12	13	14	15	16	17
18	19	20	21	22	23	24
25	26	27	28	29	30	

Iyyar						
S	M	T	W	T	F	S
						1
2	3	4	5	6	7	8
9	10	11	12	13	14	15
16	17	18	19	20	21	22
23	24	25	26	27	28	29

period of time...a Leap year). The Antichrist will arise on *Iyyar 10.*

The Tribulation Period will begin on Nisan 15 because the 1st half of Daniels 70th week ended on Nisan 14. After a *gap in time* it will resume on Nisan 15 at an unknown future point in time. Iyyar 10 is 25 days into the the Tribulation period of 1267 days (1242+25) = 1267 Days. The Great Tribulation will begin when Satan is cast down to the earth (Revelation 12) and the Antichrist will arise 25 days later (compare Revelation 12:9 to 13: 1-5).

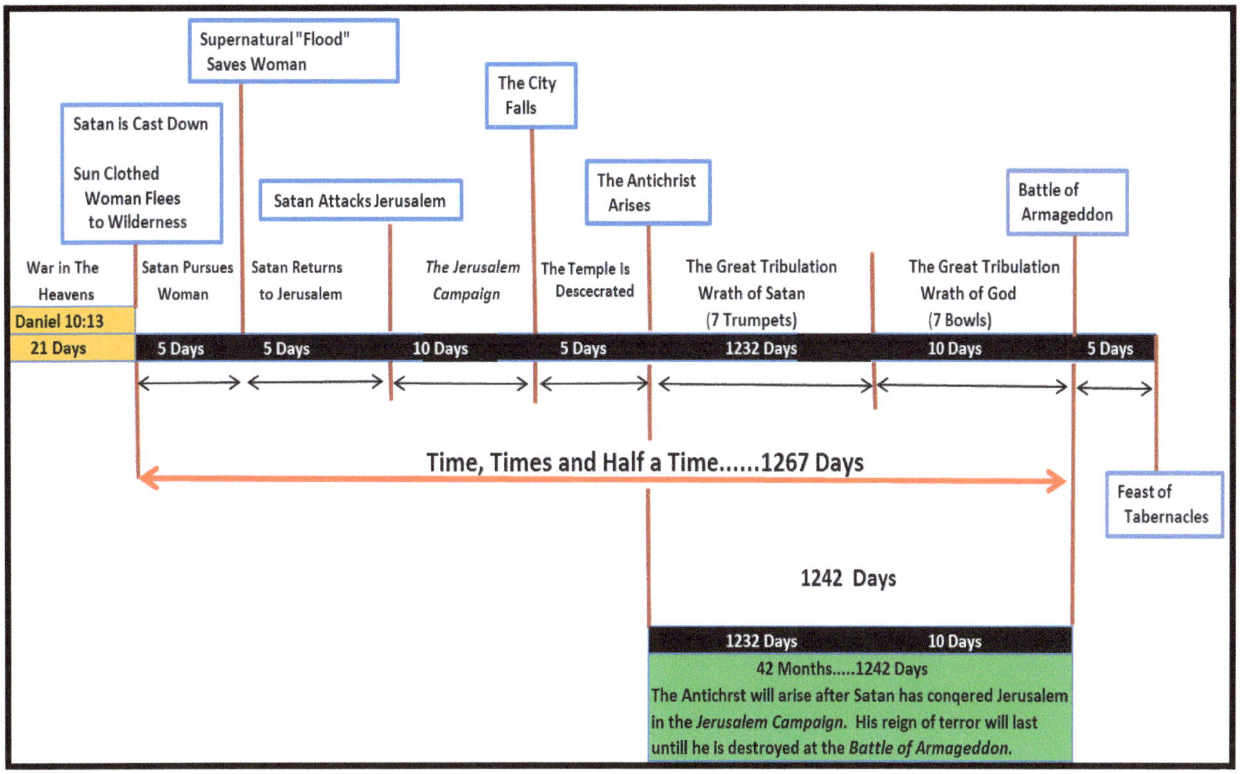

The Rebuilt Temple Will Be Descecrated for 42 Months

Time Period	Start	Finish	Scriptural Reference
42 Months	The Rebuilt Temple will be taken over by Antichrist	The Jewish Temple will be tread Underfoot by Gentiles for 42 Months	Revelation 11:2

[1] *And there was given me a reed like unto a rod: and the angel stood, saying, Rise, and measure the temple of God, and the altar, and them that worship therein.*
[2] *But the court which is without the temple leave out, and measure it not; for it is given unto the Gentiles: and the holy city shall they tread under foot* ***forty and two months***
Revelation 11: 1-2

In Revelation 11: 1-2 John is approached by *an angel* who gives him a *reed* which is a measuring stick that resembles a *rod*. John is told to go and measure the *Temple and the Alter* therein, but do not measure the *outer court* because it is given over to the Gentiles. Herod's Temple had an inner court and an outer court. The gentiles could visit the temple but they could go no further than the outer court. The context of this command is to understand that the gentiles who are in view here are the ungodly followers of Satan and anyone who is not in Jesus Christ. The analogy is not totally clear, since Satan and the antichrist will invade the temple and sit inside as God. The *holy city* is almost certainly the earthly City of Jerusalem which after Satan has attacked Jerusalem in the Armageddon Campaign will control and rule over Jerusalem. It is not uncommon to hear prophecy teachers claim that the Holy Temple that was destroyed by Rome in 70 AD would never be rebuilt. Revelation 11: 1-2 completely destroys this concept. Before the last 3.5 years of Great Tribulation can take place the Jerusalem Temple will certainly be rebuilt. The Jews will also resume temple worship and sacrifices as a part of Satan's *Covenant with Death* (Isaiah 28:15, Daniel 11:31). This will all cease when the Satanically indwelled Antichrist will enter the temple and declare himself as God (Daniel 9:27).

It is not uncommon to hear prophecy teachers claim that the Holy Temple that was destroyed by Rome in 70 AD would never be rebuilt. Revelation 11: 1-2 completely destroy this concept. Before the last 3.5 years of Great Tribulation can take place the Jerusalem Temple will be rebuilt. The Jews will also resume temple worship and sacrifices as a part of Satan's *Covenant with Death*. This will all cease when the Antichrist will enter the temple and declare himself as God. When the antichrist is cast down to earth the last half of Daniel's 70th week will begin. Satan will persecute all who refuse to worship him in the form of the antichrist. Satan is a created angel who must have a body within which to dwell. The Antichrist will be Satan incarnate and the False prophet will establish an apostate, worldwide religious system.

The antichrist will persecute the Jews and Christians for 1242 days which is called 42 months in Revelation 11:2. The Holy Scriptures never state that 42 months is 1242 days. *Where did this come from?* We know that the rebuilt temple will be trodden underfoot by Gentiles (unbelievers and followers of Satan) for 42 months. The Age of Grace will not end until Satan is destroyed at the Battle of Armageddon on Tishri 10 (Feast of Yom Kippur). During this current age there will be only two types of people: Those who believe in the Lord Jesus Christ (Christians) and those who do not. Salvation is now offered to Jews and Gentiles alike. Unbelievers are also composed of Jews and Gentiles. We know when the 42 months will end...at the Battle of Armageddon. The duration of these 42 months can be determined by "walking" backward through 24 months on the Jewish calendar, counting one month at a time from Tishri 10. 42 months prior to Tishri 10 is *Iyyar 10.* This is the day that the antichrist will enter into the temple, declare himself to be God and demand to be worshipped. All who refuse to do so will be martyred and all who capitulate will receive the Mark of the Beast on their right hand or forehead (Revelation 13: 14-18). That mark is generally believed to be the number 666, which is the *number of a man* (Revelation 13:18).

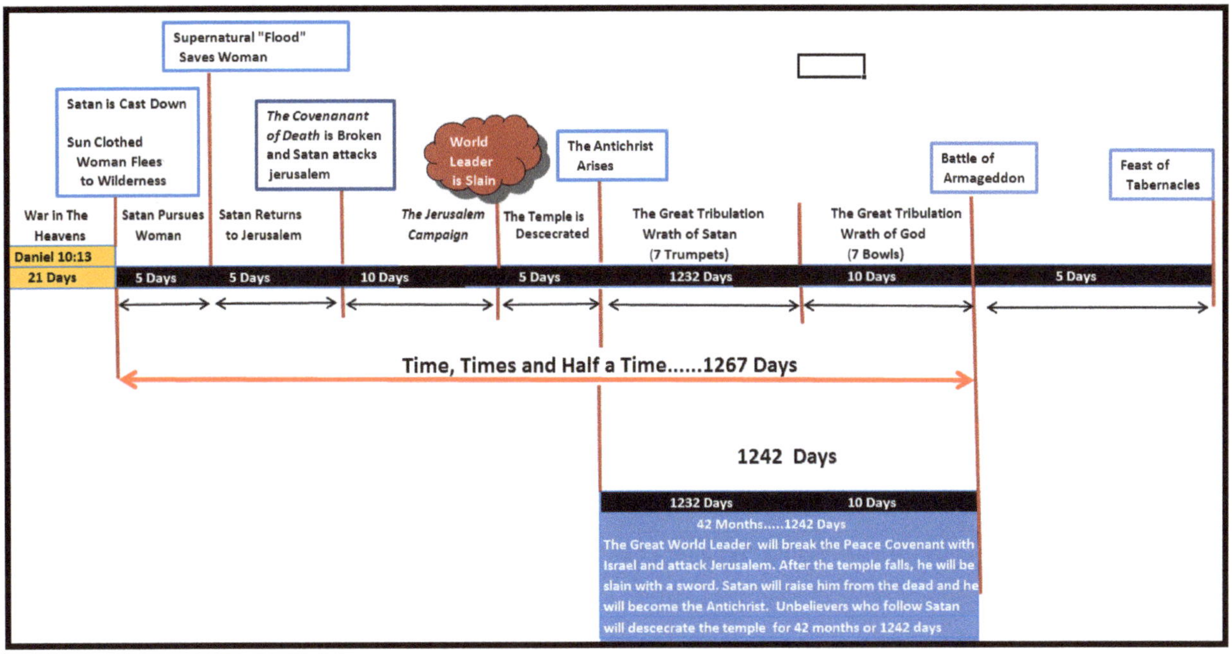

Two Witnesses Will Prophesy For 1260 Days

1260 Days 1260 Days	Two Witnesses will Start Prophesying	They will prophesy until the Saints (Jews and Gentiles) are Raptured. They will then be killed and lay in street 3.5 days. God will then say: "Come up Here"	Revelation 11:3

[3] *And I will give power unto my two witnesses, and they shall prophesy a* ***thousand two hundred and threescore days****, clothed in sackcloth.*

[4] *These are the two olive trees, and the two candlesticks standing before the God of the earth.*

[5] *And if any man will hurt them, fire proceedeth out of their mouth, and devours their enemies: and if any man will hurt them, he must in this manner be killed.*

[6] *These have power to shut heaven, that it rain not in the days of their prophecy: and have power over waters to turn them to blood, and to smite the earth with all plagues, as often as they will.*

[7] *And when they shall have finished their testimony, the beast that ascends out of the*

bottomless pit shall make war against them, and shall overcome them, and kill them.
[**8**] *And their dead bodies shall lie in the street of the great city, which spiritually is called Sodom and Egypt, where also our Lord was crucified.*
[**9**] *And they of the people and kindreds and tongues and nations shall see their dead bodies three days and an half, and shall not suffer their dead bodies to be put in graves.*
[**10**] *And they that dwell upon the earth shall rejoice over them, and make merry, and shall send gifts one to another; because these two prophets tormented them that dwelt on the earth.*
[**11**] *And after three days and an half the Spirit of life from God entered into them, and they stood upon their feet; and great fear fell upon them which saw them.*
[**12**] *And they heard a great voice from heaven saying unto them, Come up hither. And they ascended up to heaven in a cloud; and their enemies beheld them* Revelation 11: 3-12

When the Antichrist will arise and demand that He will be worshipped as God, two witnesses will be divinely appointed by God to hold fast.... face tribulation....and do not be afraid because those who do not capitulate to the demands of the Antichrist may be martyred, but they will inherit eternal life in they are faithful.

The two witnesses will be anninted and preach for 1260 days. They will be clothed in *sackcloth* and receive *great power*. Their message will be: *Do not worship the beast*, no matter what the consequences might be of *not* doing so. There are two specific warnings: (1) Do not take the mark of the beast and (2) Do not worship the graven image of the Antichrist.

The Antichhrist will demand that all who live upon the earth will worship him and him alone. Yhe antichrist is neither omnipotent or omnicence; he cannot be all over the world and threten people everywhere to capitulate or die. *How can this possibly come to pass?* Immediately folowing the arise of the antichrist, Satan will supernaturally initiate another evil person which we call the *False Prophet*. The false prophet will be appointed the world leader of a universal "church" which will worship Satan. He imitates Christ and appears as a *Lamb* but he speaks as a *dragon*.

[**11**] *And I beheld another beast coming up out of the earth; and he had two horns like a lamb, and he spoke as a dragon.*
[**12**] *And he exercises all the power of the first beast before him, and causes the earth and them which dwell therein to worship the first beast, whose deadly wound was healed.*
[**13**] *And he doeth great wonders, so that he maketh fire come down from heaven on the earth in the sight of men,*
[**14**] *And deceives them that dwell on the earth by the means of those miracles which he had power to do in the sight of the beast; saying to them that dwell on the earth, that they should make an image to the beast, which had the wound by a sword, and did live.*

[**15**] *And he had power to give life unto the image of the beast, that the image of the beast should both speak, and cause that as many as would not worship the image of the beast should be killed* Revelation 13: 11-15

At this point, the scriptures reveal a fact that is seldom if ever taught by any prophecy teacher. It is with great sorrow that the following truth is now fully revealed. he has been given unlimeted power by Satan (Revelation 13: 12, 14). He causes fire to come down from the skyand performs miracles. The most deadly power that he possesses is that he will make an image of the beast (antichrist) and incredibly it will come to life...it will actually speak and command all in the sound of the image's voice to worship the antichist or *die* (Revelation 13:15). This is how the antichrist will appear before all who live in Israel, other countries and other continents (Revelation 12:17). it is no wonder that Christ declared: *And except those days should be shortened, there should no flesh be saved: but for the elect's sake those days shall be shortened* (Matthew 24:22). *How will those days be shortened*? The elect will be raptured out, but not before the entire Tribulation begins. *How could days be shortened if the elect never had to endure any of them?* The elect will be raptured out as the 7th trumpet sounds. The *shortened days* are the days during which the *Wrath of God is poured out upon the desolate*. This is called a pre-wrath rapture. It is fully developed by Phillips; The Book of Revelation: *Mysteries Revealed*. Those who may be skeptical and have been indoctrinated into what is called a *Pre-Tribulation Rapture* should read Revelation 11: 15-18, Revelation 12:17 and Revelation 15: 1-8.

Those who choose to follow after Satan will be *marked* in their *right hand* or in their *foreheads*. It is commonly assumed that this mark is the number 666 (Revelation 13:8). Those who escape will not be allowed to buy or sell anything without this *mark* (Revelation 13:17).

[**16**] *And he causes all, both small and great, rich and poor, free and bond, to receive a mark in their right hand, or in their foreheads:*
[**17**] *And that no man might buy or sell, save he that had the mark, or the name of the beast, or the number of his name* Revelation 13: 6-7

There are also eternal consequences for those who take the mark of the beast.

And the beast was taken, and with him the false prophet that wrought miracles before him, with which he deceived them that had received the mark of the beast, and them that worshipped his image. These both were cast alive into a lake of fire burning with brimstone Revelation 19:20

For those who refuse to worship Satan and refuse the mark, there are great rewards.

And I saw thrones, and they sat upon them, and judgment was given unto them: and I saw the souls of them that were beheaded for the witness of Jesus, and for the word of God, and which had not worshipped the beast, neither his image, neither had received his mark upon their foreheads, or in their hands; and they lived and reigned with Christ a thousand years
Revelation 20:4

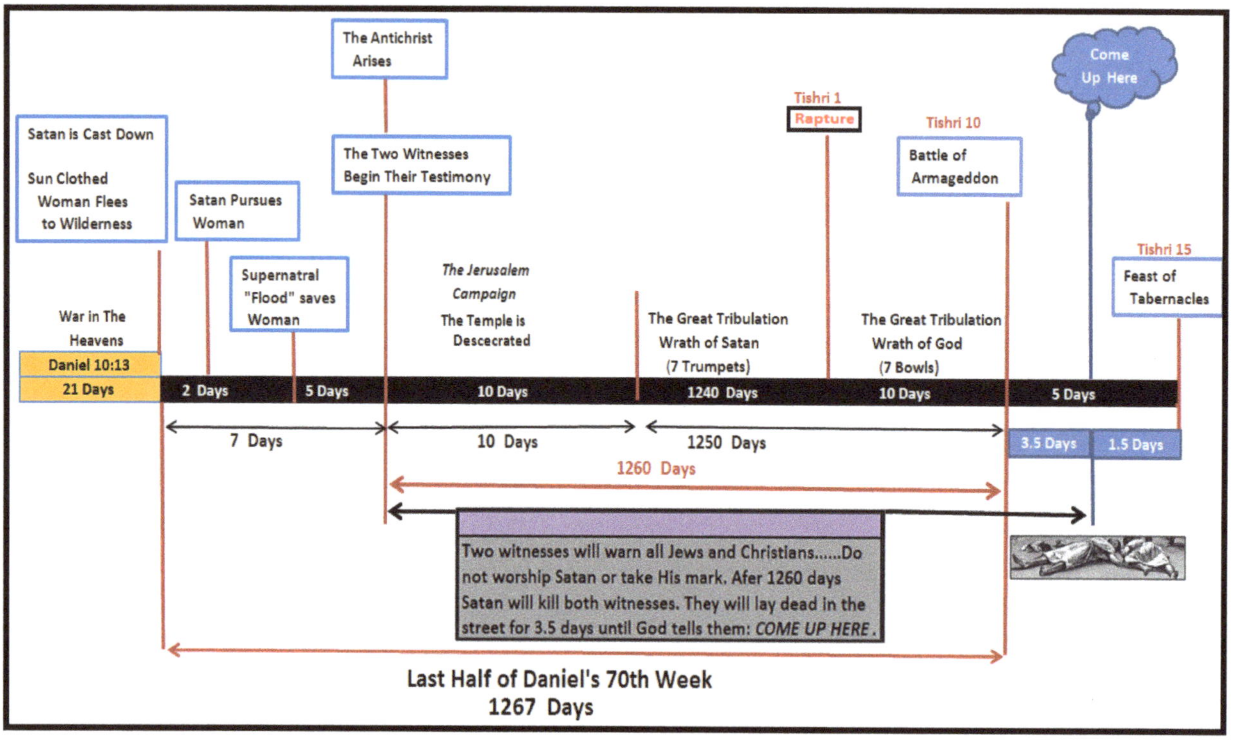

The Woman is Fed in A Place Prepared by for 1260 Days

Time Period	Start	Finish	Scrriptural Reference
1260 Days	Woman is Fed in A Place Prepared by God	Until Jesus Comes For Them After Battle of Armageddon	Revelation 12:6

And the woman fled into the wilderness, where she hath a place prepared of God, that they should feed her there a thousand two hundred and threescore days Revelation 12:6

The *woman* has previously been identified as *Israel* who is the mother of us all. The apostle Paul revealed: *Know ye therefore that they which are of faith, the same are the children of Abraham* (Galatians 3:7). Those who fled into the wilderness are often identified as only the Jews, but this is unlikely since when God supernaturally protected the *woman* Satan turned to persecute the *remnant of her seed*. It is also possible that a remnant of her seed is the 144,000 (12,000 from 12 tribes of Israel) who have previously been sealed against Tribulation Wrath. However, this is not likely. Why would these 144,000 be sealed if they are going to be protected in the wilderness?

...the dragon was wroth with the woman, and went to make war with the remnant of her seed, which keep the commandments of God, and have the testimony of Jesus Christ
Revelation 12:17

How is this woman nourished? It is not clear how the woman is nourished, but two possibilities can be postulated. God is quite capable of feeding and protecting those who He chooses. The Children of Israel were nourished by manna and quail for 4years in the wilderness. Elijah was fed by raven after he fled in fear from Jezebel, and King David was nourished when He hid from

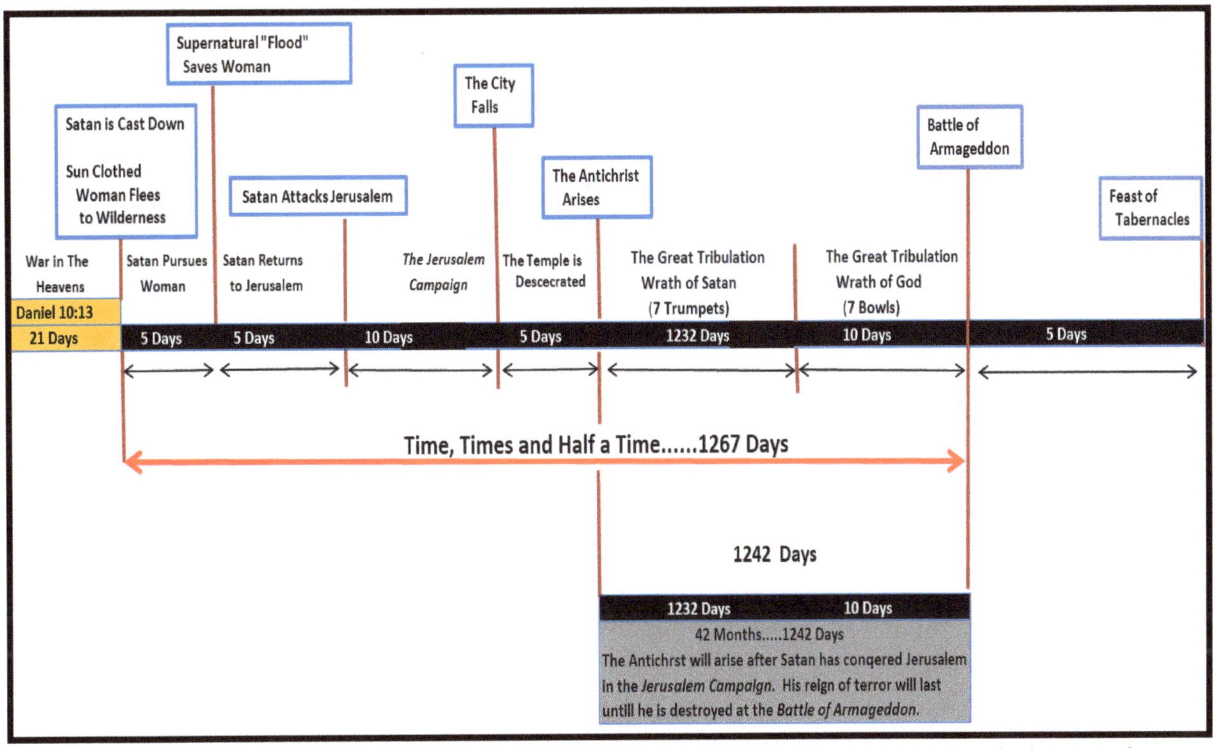

Saul in a remote cave. The other possibility is that this remnant fled to a special place in the wilderness where they were fed and protected by those who lived there. Many have proposed that they fled to the city of *Petra*. Those who would protect this remnant might be a part of the Sheep in the *Judgment of the Sheep and Goats* following the Battle of Armageddon. The starting point of this protection is when this remnant flees from the City of Jerusalem before and during the *Jerusalem Campaign*. Christ warned the Jewish people to flee quickly when the Temple is desecrated by the antichrist in His *Olivet Discourse* (Matthew 24: 15-21). This group will need to be protected until Satan, the Antichrist and the False Prophet are all captured and condemned by Christ at the Battle of Armageddon.

The Woman is Nourished in the Wilderness for a Time, Times and Half a Time

Time, Times and Half a Time **1267 Days**	The Woman (Israel) of Revelation 12 is nourished in the wilderness from the dragon (Satan)	The Jews in the wilderness will be nourished to keep them alive so that they can enter the Millennial Kingdom and inherit the Promised land	Revelation 12:14

[**13**] *And when the dragon saw that he was cast unto the earth, he persecuted the woman which brought forth the man child.*
[**14**] *And to the woman were given two wings of a great eagle, that she might fly into the wilderness, into her place, where she is nourished for a* ***time, and times, and half a time****, from the face of the serpent*
[**15**] *And the serpent cast out of his mouth water as a flood after the woman, that he might cause her to be carried away of the flood.*
[**16**] *And the earth helped the woman, and the earth opened her mouth, and swallowed up the* flood which the dragon cast out of his mouth.
[**17**] *And the dragon was wroth with the woman, and went to make war with the remnant of her seed, which keep the commandments of God, and have the testimony of Jesus Christ.*
Revelation 12: 13-17

The woman which will *fly into the wilderness* (not literally, but quickly) is assumed by all prophecy teachers as the same woman seen in Revelation 12:6, and that would directly equate a time, time and half a time to 1260 days. In Revelation 12: 15-16 additional information is revealed concerning how the fleeing remant is saved from the pursuing Satan. The old serpent (Satan/the Dragon) evidently attempts to destroy all who are fleeing from Jerusalem with a great flood of water (Revelation 12:15). Satan obviousy intends to drown those fleeing just as the army of the Pharogh was destroyed by water at the Exodus in the Red Sea. However, God will save His people (agin) by supernatural means. The earth will *open* and *swallow up the flood.*

Satan is absolutely furious.....He has been cast out of heaven and confined to this earth, the Man-Child has escaped him, and now those who flee from him have been supernaturally saved. He is *wroth with the woman*. In the Greek the word wroth is *orge* and it literally means to be furious or angry. There are two Greek words which ar used in this context.....*orge* and *thumas*. Thumas is a deep anger which is controlled. Orge is like a teapot which explodes. Satan is furious, and he now turns upon another remnant of her seed: *the remnant of her seed which keep the commandments of God, and have the testimony of Jesus Christ* (Revelation 12:17).

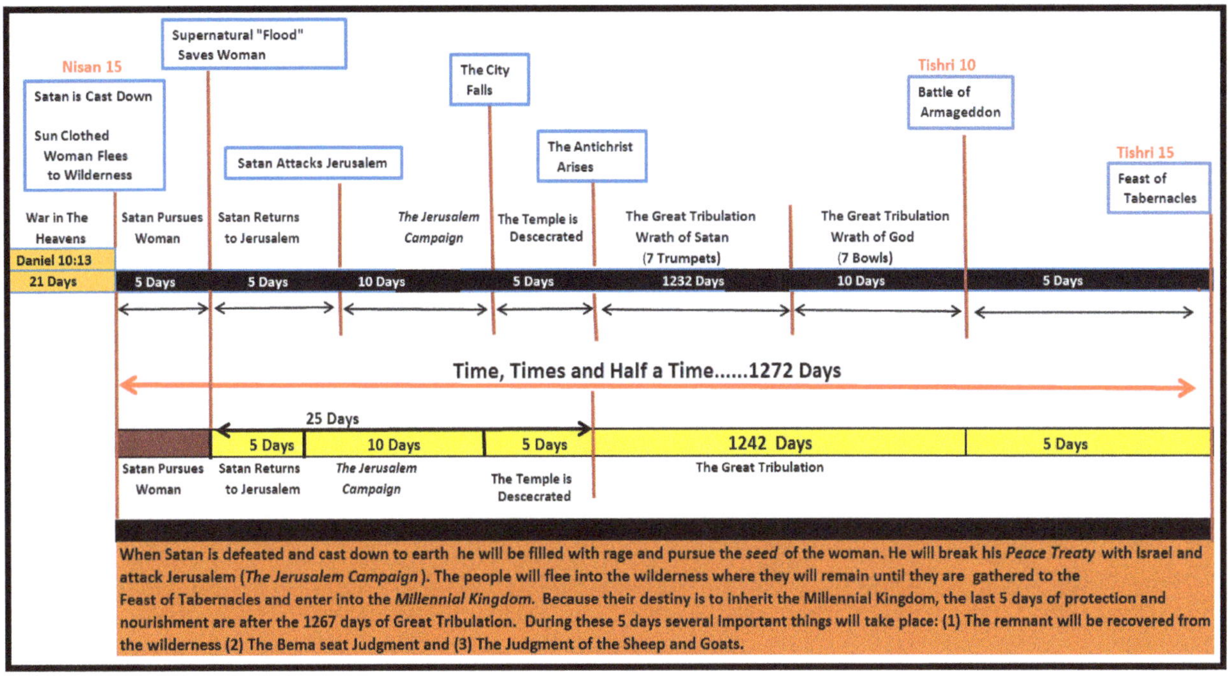

Exegesis

There are two separate references to the *woman* of Revelation 12 being protected supernaturally by God.

And the woman fled into the wilderness, where she hath a place prepared of God, that they should feed her there a ***thousand two hundred and threescore days*** Revelation 12:6

And to the woman were given two wings of a great eagle, that she might fly into the wilderness, into her place, where she is nourished for a ***time, and times, and half a time****, from the face of the serpent* Revelation 12:14

The common interpretation is that Revelation 12:14 is a re-statement of Revelation 12:6. This is not true and the 1260 days of Revelation 12:6 cannot be equated to the time, times and half-a-time of Revelation 12:14. This conclusion can only be reached by carefully considering the context of both statements. The 1260 days in Revelation 12:6 is a simple statement that God will protect the woman (Revelation 12:17) in the wilderness for 1260 days. Zechariah refers to this time of great tribulation among the Jews, in which two-thirds of them will die when Satan breaks the peace treaty with Israel and invades Jerusalem. Only one-third will manage to escape to a safe refuge in the wilderness – most likely to the ancient City of Petra.

[**1**] *Behold, the day of the LORD cometh, and thy spoil shall be divided in the midst of thee.*
[**2**] *For I will gather all nations against Jerusalem to battle; and the city shall be taken, and the houses rifled, and the women ravished; and half of the city shall go forth into captivity, and the residue of the people shall not be cut off from the city* Zechariah 14: 1-2

[**8**] *And it shall come to pass, that in all the land, saith the LORD, two parts therein shall be cut off and die; but the third shall be left therein.*
[**9**] *And I will bring the third part through the fire, and will refine them as silver is refined, and will try them as gold is tried: they shall call on my name, and I will hear them: I will say, It is my people: and they shall say, The LORD is my God* Zechariah 13: 8-9

The woman in Revelation 12 will be supernaturally protected for 1260 days, and fed by the *sheep* of Matthew 25:35. This is identical to the duration of the Antichrist persecution (1260 days). Revelation 12:14 is immediately followed by:

[**15**] *And the serpent cast out of his mouth water as a flood after the woman, that he might cause her to be carried away of the flood.*
[**16**] *And the earth helped the woman, and the earth opened her mouth, and swallowed up the flood which the dragon cast out of his mouth* Revelation 12: 15-16

As soon as the *man child* (Phillips: The Book of Revelation; *Mysteries Revealed*) is birthed, the *woman* from which the man child comes (Revelation 12:17) is attacked by Satan. The woman flees to the wilderness (Revelation 12:6) and is pursued by Satan (Revelation 12: 12-13). Just as Satan is about to devour the believing remnant with a flood of water (Revelation 12:17), God intervenes. He opens up a great crevasse in the earth that *swallows up the flood*. Satan is furious, and he turns to make war for the rest of the Tribulation Period against all Jews and Christians. He attacks Jerusalem, energizes the Antichrist and the false prophet and assumes control of the temple.... This will take 7 days....1267 days (time, times and half-a-time) minus 1260 days(reign of Antichrist). Careful examination of Revelation 12:14 reveals that this period of time (1260 days) is only the period of time that the remnant is protected *in the wilderness* (1260 days), and that Revelation 12: 13-14 refers to a longer period of time which begins as soon as the woman berths the man-child, and includes her miraculous rescue from Satan when the earth opens up and consumes the flood of Satan. This is a longer period of time (1267) days that that given in Revelation 12:6. This is precisely why God used two different time references in 8 verse of scripture.

This analysis of the last 1267 days of the Tribulation Period is new, and assumes that 42 months, time, times and half-a-time are not all 1260 days. These durations of time have been determined in context using scriptural clues. Other time periods are "best guess" estimates. This analysis assumes a 3.5 year tribulation and not a 7 year tribulation. In either case, the analysis is valid and might provide insight into the last half of Daniel's 70th week.

Revelation 12:6 "And the woman fled into the wilderness, where she hath a place prepared of God, that they should feed her there a thousand two hundred and threescore days."

https://www.slideshare.net/nich777/176982124-revelation12

Chapter 4

The Death of Jesus Christ

The Crucifixion of our Lord Jesus Christ

Daniel 9: 24-27 has been interpreted and explained in Chapters 1 and 2, and It has been determined that a decree was issued by Nebuchadnezzar to Ezra in his 7th year of reign (September of 458 BC to September of 457 BC), and that Jesus Christ came to the river Jordan in the Fall of 26 AD where He was baptized and began His ministry of reconciliation to the Jews. After a 3.5 year ministry He was crucified on Wednesday, Nisan 14 in 30 AD. Evidence has been presented which strongly suggests that the Jewish Calendar in use today is ancient in origin and likely was given to Moses at Mount Sinai. God spoke to Moses and gave him detailed instructions on how to build the Tabernacle and all of its furniture, and exactly when to observe the Seven Feasts of Israel each year. The Biblical records never specifically say how long Christ taught, healed and conducted His ministry as God in the flesh. There has been substantial research as to when Jesus Christ was born, started His earthly ministry and died (Phillips; *The Birth and Death of Jesus Christ*, Phillips: *The Birth of Jesus*: *A Forensic Analysis,* Coulter, Fred R., The Day Jesus the Christ Died). This research and that conducted by many other bible scholars have suggested that Jesus came to the River Jordan on the *Feast of Tabernacles* on Tishri 1 in September of 30 AD at *about the age of 30.* This investigation accepts those conclusions. Most reliable and authoritative sources conclude that Christ had a 3.5 year ministry during which there were 4 Passover Feasts. The Apostle John wrote his Gospel following a timeline built around these 4 feasts.

1.0 **The 1st Passover**

And the Jews' Passover was at hand, and Jesus went up to Jerusalem John 2:13

2.0 **The 2nd Passover**

After this there was a feast of the Jews; and Jesus went up to Jerusalem John 5:1
John doesn't record which feast is being attended, but some of the early manuscripts use a "the" in front of the word "feast" leading scholars to conclude that it was probably the Passover feast. Of all the possibilities, the Passover feast fits best with the available evidence.

3.0 **The 3rd Passover**

[3] *And Jesus went up into a mountain, and there he sat with his disciples.*
[**4**] *And the Passover, a feast of the Jews, was nigh* John 6: 3-4

It is not clear whether or not Jesus attended this Passover in Jerusalem, but it is likely that He did

4.0 The 4th Passover

[55] *And the Jews Passover was nigh at hand: and many went out of the country up to Jerusalem before the Passover, to purify themselves.*
[56] *Then sought they for Jesus, and spoke among themselves, as they stood in the temple, What think ye, that he will not come to the feast?* John 11: 55-56

Whether or not Jesus *attended* all four Passover Feasts during His earthly ministry is simply scholarly debate. The important conclusion is that there were 4 Passover seasons during the 3.5 year ministry of Christ. It is interesting that some have concluded that Christ only had a 1 or 2 year ministry which is impossible.

The 4th Passover recorded by John was when He went to Jerusalem to be crucified. All prophecy scholars and preachers agree that the Jewish date of the crucifixion was Nisan 14, but as we have previously discussed the day of the week and the year are both highly disputed. All agree that Christ was crucified between 30 AD and 34 AD. The year 30 AD is the year that best fits all Biblical records. It is interesting and possibly significant that the Passover of Nisan 14, 30 AD was half way between the beginning and end of Daniel's 70th week and that Wednesday is in the middle of the last week as required by Daniel 9: 26-27.

There are four feasts that all Jewish men are required to attend(Deuteronomy 16:16): *Passover* (Nisan 14), *Feast of Unleavened Bread* (Nisan 15-21), the *Feast of Pentecost*, and the *Feast of Tabernacles* (Tishri 15-22).

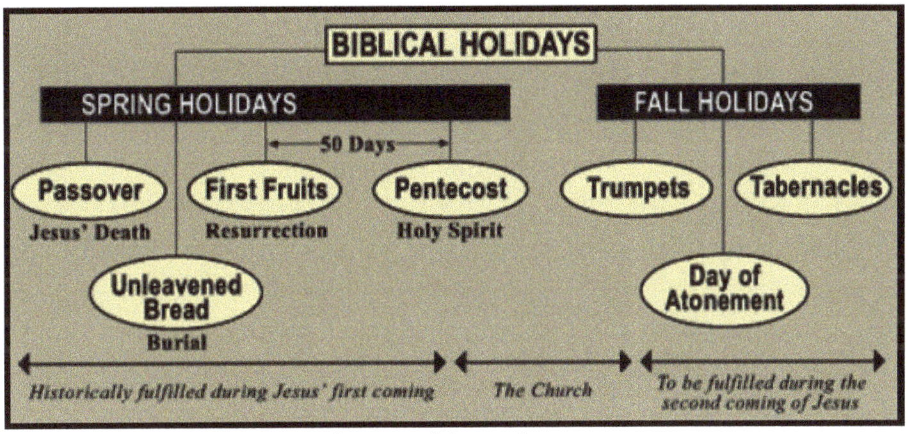

www.WatchmanBiblestudy.com

All four of the spring Feasts hold great significance to the salvation and redemption to Jews and gentiles alike. The *Feast of Passover* was when Jesus Christ died for the sins of Jews and gentiles alike. The *Feast of Firstfruits* was when Jesus Christ ascended to heaven and presented

Himself as the perfect sacrificial Lamb of God who was the final and complete sacrifice for sins. The *Feast of Unleavened Bread* is a shadow and type of Jesus Christ. He is the *Bread of Life*, pure and sinless without *leaven* (a type of sin). *Pentecost* was when the Holy Spirit first fell on all believers. When Christ died, the Old Covenant sacrificial system for the atonement of sins was *finished* (John 19:30). God wanted every male Jew to see these things with their own eyes. Finally, the redemption of all Jews (and Gentiles) will not be complete until all of those Old Covenant Jews who died in the faith of Abraham and all New Covenant Christians (the Ecclesia) are resurrected or caught up alive at the rapture of all believers...alive or dead. Forgiveness of sin (justification), righteousness in Jesus Christ (sanctification) and the transformation of our earthly tabernacle (body) into an undefiled and corruptible body (glorification) are all evidenced and guaranteed in our Lord Jesus Christ.

The Daniel Prophecy specifically reveals that **after threescore and two weeks** (after 483 years had been completed), then Christ would be ***cut off*** (crucified). Exactly when this would occur is easily determined: It was on ***Nisan 14, 30 AD*** on a ***Wednesday***, which is the ***Feast of Passover***. The offered chronology points to this date, but is there other evidence that this is the correct year? The answer is, ***YES***.

Nisan 14, 30 AD is the Correct Date And Year

- The Apostle Paul was converted on the road to Damascus by Jesus Christ, who appeared in his risen body shortly after he was crucified; which we have just shown is in 30 AD. Fourteen (14) years after his conversion, Paul records in Galatians 2:1 that He, Barnabus and Titus journeyed to Jerusalem. While Paul, Barnabus and Titus were in Jerusalem, King Herod Agrippa died. This date is known to be during or shortly after the Passover Feast of 44 BC (March/April). Josephus confirms this in Antiq. xix 8.2. If 14 years are subtracted from March/April of 44 AD, we arrive at March/April of 30 AD as we have shown.
- The Apostle Luke records that John the Baptist came to the River Jordan baptizing and preaching repentance in the 15th year of Tiberius Caesar. (Luke 3:1-3). Tiberius was the successor to Augustus Caesar, who became the Emperor of Rome on Jan 13, 27 BC After the assassination of Julius Caesar. The last five years of his life (AD 10-14) were untroubled by war or disaster. Augustus was ageing fast, and was more and more disinclined to appear personally in the senate or in public. In 12 AD he consented, reluctantly we are told, to yet one more renewal of his imperial reign for ten years. Roman emperors were appointed in January, and officially conferred in March. He consented with a demand that his stepson ***Tiberius***, now over fifty years of age should be equated with himself, both in power and authority in the administration of the empire. Tiberius then retreated to an island villa and hardly ever appeared in public between 12 AD and his death in 14 AD. Augustus died on Aug 19,

14 AD and Tiberius became sole ruler. If Luke measured the 15 years from the co-reign of Tiberius starting in the Spring of 12 BC; the 15th year would be the Spring of 26 AD to the Spring of 27 AD. Christ was baptized by John in September of 26 AD. There is no reason to think that Luke would not have counted the reign of Tiberius from 12 BC. Jerusalem was effectively under the iron boot of Tiberius between 12 AD - 14 AD, when the death of Augustus occurred.

- Just before the *first* Passover of Christ's ministry (John 2:13), after his baptism at the River Jordan, Christ foretold of his death and resurrection in three days. He said:

Jesus answered and said unto them, Destroy this temple, and in three days I will raise it up John 2:19

But the Jews thought that Christ was referring to Herod's temple and replied:

Then said the Jews, Forty and six years was this temple in building, and wilt thou rear it up in three days? John 2:20

In the works of Josephus (Book XV: 11:1), he records that construction on the temple was begun in the 18th year of King Herod's reign, which was 20 BC - 19 BC. Leaping forward 46 years, we come to 27 AD-28 AD. The *first* Passover in Jesus ministry was in March/April of 27 BC.

- Jesus was "about 30 years of age" when He was baptized. If the baptism of Jesus took place in September of 26 AD, he would have been born around September of 5 BC (remember to subtract one year when crossing from BC to AD). Until recently, everyone believed that Herod died in the Spring of 4 BC. A new theory places the death of Herod in either 1 BC or 1 AD, but that date is not without controversy for all but those who wish to show a Friday crucifixion in 33 AD. If Herod died in 4 BC, then Christ could not have been born after that date. In a detailed study of the Birth of Christ, Phillips has shown using astronomical and NASA data, biblical clues, the records of Josephus and service of 24 courses of priests between 70 AD and 5 BC that Christ was born in 5 BC. If Christ was born in the Fall of 5 BC He would be *about 30 years of Age* (Luke 3:23) in the Fall of 26 AD when He began His 3.5 year ministry.
- Shortly before the last Passover of Christ's ministry at which He was crucified, Jesus was delivering the Olivet Discourse to his disciples at which time he prophesied that Herod's Temple would be destroyed and when it would come to pass.

> *Verily I say unto you, this generation shall not pass till all these things be fulfilled*
> Matthew 24:34

This was in the Spring of 30 AD. Almost all biblical scholars agree that based upon the Exodus account where the entire generation of Hebrews who left Egypt would perish (die), a biblical generation was 40 years. Adding 40 years to the Spring of 30 AD, we arrive in the Spring of 70 AD, when Herod's temple was destroyed. Only a 30 AD crucifixion renders this destruction in exactly one generation.

- All biblical scholars agree that Christ died between 30 AD and 34 AD. All agree that He died on Nisan 14 at the Feast of Passover. However, there is widespread disagreement as to whether Christ was crucified on a Wednesday on a Wednesday, Thursday or Friday. There are millions of Christians, pastors and teachers who aggressively declare that Christ died on a Friday in 33 AD (J. Dwight Pentecost, *The Life and Times of Jesus Christ*) and there are millions more who believe that Christ Died on a Thursday in 32 AD (Sir Robert Anderson, *The Coming Prince*). All have one thing in common they deny that the Holy Scriptures are infallible by denying that Jesus Christ would lie in the grave for 3 full days and 3 full nights before He would be resurrected...by his own words (Matthew 12:40, Matthew 27:63, Mark 8:31, Mark 14:58). Perhaps Jesus the Son of God was confused...perhaps He did not tell the truth....perhaps He only used the Sign of Jonah to confound the Jews....NONSENSE. This is such an important theological issue that it needs to be investigated. In the following section, it will be proved that Christ was in the tomb for a full 3 days and 3 nights just as He said He would be, and that he must have died on a Wednesday.

The Seven Feasts of Israel and The Seven High Holy Days

The Key to understanding how long Christ was in the grave is to understand that His death, burial and resurrection completely fulfilled Old Testament prophecy and exactly satisfied the 4 Spring feasts of Israel.

Each of these 7 Feasts of Israel were to be observed for two reasons: (1) To commemorate and remember how God freed His chosen people from Egyptian slavery and to (2) Teach of the 1st and 2nd comings of our Lord Jesus Christ. Each of the 7 feasts was called a *moed*. The Hebrew word *moed* means a *rehearsal* or an *appointment*. There were 4 Spring feasts and 3 Fall feasts. The 1st four spring feasts were completely fulfilled at the first coming of Jesus Christ. The last three feasts have yet to be fulfilled but will be at the end of the age.

In addition to the 7 Feasts of Israel, God ordained 7 special Sabbath days which accompany 5 of the 7 Holy Feasts. These are called *High Sabbath Days*. The following table summarizes each of the High Holy Days. These 7 High Sabbath Days are seldom studied and sometimes completely unknown to the average Christian. The High Sabbath day of Nisan 15 took place shortly after the crucifixion of Jesus Christ and His late afternoon burial on Wednesday, Nisan 14. Like all other Jewish calendar days, each of these 7 Feast Days can occur on different days of the week in any one year.

The 7 High Sabbath Days (*Leviticus 23*)

1	First Day of Feast of Unleavened Bread	Nisan 15
2	Last Day of Feast of Unleavened Bread	Nisan 21
3	Pentecost.... 50 Days After the Only Weekly Sabbath That Occurs During the Feast of Unleavened Bread	
4	The Feast Of Trumpets (Rosh Hashanah)	Tishri 1
5	The Feast of Atonement (Yom Kippur)	Tishri 10
6	The First Day of the Feast of Tabernacles (Succoth)	Tishri 15
7	The Last (Great) Day of Feast of Tabernacles	Tishri 22

The 7 Feasts of Israel and the 7 High Holy days should be carefully studied to fully understand biblical prophecy (Chapter 3). In some ways the 7 High Sabbath Days are considered to be more holy than the weekly Sabbath day of Saturday, since they occur only 7 times a year. We will shortly see that *High Sabbath Days* will play a critical role in determining when Jesus Christ was crucified. In Particular, the High Sabbath Day associated with the 1st day of the Feast of Unleavened Bread (Nisan 15) will prove to be extremely important. The following table illustrates the 7 Feasts of Israel and their meaning to all Christians.

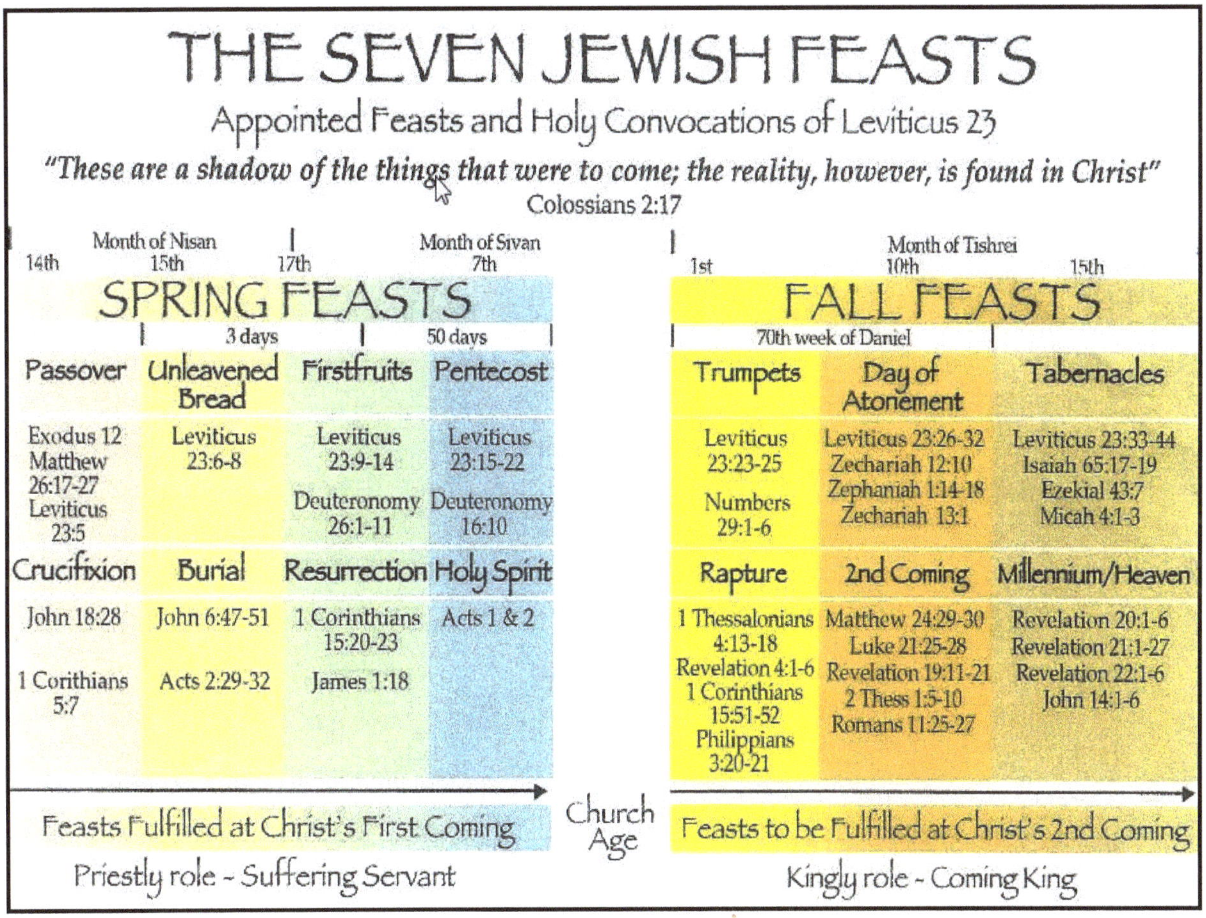

THE SEVEN JEWISH FEASTS
Appointed Feasts and Holy Convocations of Leviticus 23
"These are a shadow of the things that were to come; the reality, however, is found in Christ"
Colossians 2:17
Month of Nisan
14th
15th
17th
Month of Sivan
7th
Month of Tishrei
1st
10th
15th
SPRING FEASTS
3 days
50 days
FALL FEASTS
70th week of Daniel
Passover
Unleavened Bread
Firstfruits
Pentecost
Trumpets
Day of Atonement
Tabernacles
Exodus 12
Matthew 26:17-27
Leviticus 23:5
Leviticus 23:6-8
Leviticus 23:9-14
Deuteronomy 26:1-11
Leviticus 23:15-22
Deuteronomy 16:10
Leviticus 23:23-25
Numbers 29:1-6
Leviticus 23:26-32
Zechariah 12:10
Zephaniah 1:14-18
Zechariah 13:1
Leviticus 23:33-44
Isaiah 65:17-19
Ezekial 43:7
Micah 4:1-3
Crucifixion
Burial
Resurrection
Holy Spirit
Rapture
2nd Coming
Millennium/Heaven
John 18:28
1 Corithians 5:7
John 6:47-51
Acts 2:29-32
1 Corinthians 15:20-23
James 1:18
Acts 1 & 2
1 Thessalonians 4:13-18
Revelation 4:1-6
1 Corinthians 15:51-52
Philippians 3:20-21
Matthew 24:29-30
Luke 21:25-28
Revelation 19:11-21
2 Thess 1:5-10
Romans 11:25-27
Revelation 20:1-6
Revelation 21:1-27
Revelation 22:1-6
John 14:1-6
Feasts Fulfilled at Christ's First Coming
Church Age
Feasts to be Fulfilled at Christ's 2nd Coming
Priestly role - Suffering Servant
Kingly role - Coming King

How Long Did Jesus Christ Lay in the Grave?

The length of time that Jesus Christ lay in the tomb of Joseph of Arimathaea is central to determining both the day of the week and the year in which Jesus was crucified. In a paradoxical observation, ask any Christian how long Jesus lay in the grave and they will immediately reply: *3 days and 3 nights*. However, probing deeper into this issue: Is *3 days and 3 nights full 12 hour days and 12 hour nights*? *Do partial days and nights count as a full day*? *When would the 3 days and 3 nights start and end*? These questions will now be examined and answered.

A logical way to begin this investigation is to document and study: *How long did Jesus Christ say that He would be in the grave*? This is a straightforward question but the answer is not so obvious.

Jesus was teaching one day in a Jewish Synagogue when He was approached by the scribes and Pharisees demanding that a *sign* be given if He was the Son of God. It was not enough that He healed the sick, raised the dead and performed other miracles. Jesus said that He would only show ***one sign*** to prove that He was the Son of God, and that was the *Sign of Jonah*.

[**38**] *Then certain of the scribes and of the Pharisees answered, saying, Master, we would see a sign from thee.*
[**39**] *But he answered and said unto them, An evil and adulterous generation seeks after a sign; and* ***there shall no sign be given to it, but the sign of the prophet Jonas****:*
[**40**] *For as Jonas was three days and three nights in the whale's belly; so shall the Son of man be* ***three days and three nights in the heart of the earth****.* Matthew 12: 38-40

Recall that Jonah was an Old Testament prophet who was called by God to witness and preach repentance to the people of Nineveh. In a pious and rebellious response, Jonah refused God and sought to flee from Him in a boat across the Mediterranean Sea. As they sailed, a violent storm raged against the boat and all of its occupants. The people on the boat cried out: *Who has caused this disaster to befall us? Surely we will all be killed*. In order to save themselves the passengers cast lots to see who had caused them to befall this great persecution. Jonah was divinely identified, and to save themselves they cast him into the sea to appease God. By another divine appointment, a great fish (not necessarily a whale) swallowed Jonah, and Jonah was passed to the belly of this great fish. There is much debate over whether or not Jonah actually died in this incident, but it is our opinion that he did because it was this very incident which was a shadow and type of the death of Jesus Christ. Jonah 2:5 records that: *The waters compassed me about, even to the soul: the depth closed me round about, the weeds were wrapped about my head*. Jesus was *swallowed up in death* just as was Jonah. No one questions that Jonah was in the belly of a great fish (Matthew 12:40) for 3 full days and 3 full nights. After this specific period of time, the aquatic creature regurgitated him up on the shore of the land and He was brought back to life. Not surprisingly, Jonah then followed God's command and started a great revival in Nineveh. *Was both Jonah and Christ actually in the grave for 3 full days and 3 full nights?* It will be shown that our Lord Jesus Christ, by His own words, was resurrected from the dead by the power of God after spending 3 full days and 3 full nights in the grave. As previously stated, this was the only sign that Christ would show that He was the only begotten Son of God. In Genesis we are told exactly what constitutes a full 24 hour "day" of daylight and darkness.

[**4**] *And God saw the light, that it was good: and God divided the light from the darkness.*
[**5**] *And God called the light Day, and the darkness he called Night. And the evening and the morning were the first day* Genesis 1: 4-5

The biblical use of the word *day* can be confusing. In the western world a day is usually equated to a 24 hour duration. In Genesis, it is critical to note that God called the period of *light* a *day* and the period of *darkness* a *night*. The entire period of time containing one full cycle of darkness and light was divided into 24 time periods which were called *hours*; 12 hours of *daylight* and 12 hours of *darkness*. Christ stated that those who believed upon Him walked in light, and those that did not walked in darkness. When Christ spoke of a "day" in John 11:9 , He was speaking of a 12 hour period of *light*.
Are there not ***twelve hours in the day****? If any man walk in the day, he stumbleth not, because he seeth the light of this world* John 11:9

This is what Christ meant when He said: *Are there not twelve hours in the day?* If there are 24 hours in a complete cycle of daylight/day and darkness/night, then there are 12 hours in the night. Jesus clearly stated that He would be in the grave/tomb for 3 full days and 3 full nights or 72 consecutive hours.

For as Jonas was three days and three nights in the whale's belly; ***so shall the Son of man be three days and three nights in the heart of the earth*** Matthew 12:40

Now the LORD had prepared a great fish to swallow up Jonah. And Jonah was in the belly of the fish ***three days and three nights*** Jonah 1:17

Both Jonah 1:17 and Matthew 12:40 say: "And Jonah was in the belly of a great fish ***three days and three nights***." Jesus clearly said that as Jonah was three days and three nights in the great fish's belly, He would also be ***in the heart of the earth.*** *What does this mean*? It is obvious that Jesus meant that He would be in the tomb for 3 days and 3 nights or 72 hours. However, this means more than His body lying in a rock-hewn sepulcher. It also means a descent into a place called *Gehenna* or *Hell*, the world of the dead, which was believed to be far below the surface of the earth. Gehenna was divided into two separate sub-regions; one was called *Paradise* and the other a *Place of Torments*. Christ descended into the place called *Paradise* when He died (Luke 23:43), and there He spoke to those Jews of faith that were waiting to be redeemed. The phrase that Jesus used, *in the heart of the earth* (Matthew 12:40) is unique to this prophecy, but we can determine what it means. Paul in Ephesians 4:9 says Jesus went into the *lower* *parts of the earth.* Paul did not specifically state that Jesus descended into Paradise, and that He was there for 3 days and 3 nights, but this is the only logical conclusion based upon Luke 23:43.

The Hebrew word for *days* in Jonah 1:17 is *yom* and the word for *night* is *lailah. Three days and three nights* denote a specific, combined period of time which by Genesis 1:5 can only mean three full periods of light and 3 full periods of darkness. This is made all the more certain by observing that the expression *3 days and 3 nights* is preceded by the Hebrew word *shalosh*, which designates the cardinal number *three.* There can be little doubt that Christ meant that 3 days and 3 nights were six full periods of 12 hours duration or 72 full hours. It is true that the Hebrew term for *either* "three days" or "three nights" when used by themselves in a Hebrew sentence can be used for parts of three, but not when the expression contains **both** *three days and three nights* together. *W*hen the Hebrew conjunction *waw* (and) is used , the expression becomes even more specific.... precluding the idea of "parts" of days or parts of nights. It always means 3 full days and 3 full nights. Confirmation of this conclusion is given by the great biblical scholar Dr. E. W. Bullinger.

> The Hebrew idiom "three days" can be used for parts of three days, *but not when the word "nights is added.* By the addition of *nights*, the expression becomes more specific, precluding the idea of parts of either days or nights. Bullinger: *Companion Bible*

Consider what a respected Jewish authority, Dr. Charles Halff, who was the founder and first president of the Director of the Christian Jew Foundation in San Antonio, Texas said when asked about how the Jews counted partial days.

> People often ask: "Didn't the Jews count part of a day as a whole day or part of a night as a whole night?" Let me say this, beloved. Whenever you encounter a statement using day and night mentioned together (Matthew 12:40, Matthew 4:12) in the scriptures, it always means three full days and three full nights (Esther 4:16, I Samuel 30:12-13, Jonah 1:17). In every instance it means full days and full nights, not a part of any day or night. Dr. Charles Huff

Although it might be conceded that there are times in the Old Testament where a portion of a day was counted as a full day, it stretches the imagination too far to apply it to the death, burial and resurrection of Jesus Christ, which was typed by the story of Jonah and the whale. To even believe that Jesus Christ would make any statement which does not mean exactly what He said does serious damage to the Holy scriptures, and is just plain wrong. Jesus always meant what He said and He said what He meant.

*For as Jonas was **three** days and **three** nights in the whale's belly; so shall the Son of man be **three** days and **three** nights **in the heart of the earth*** Matthew 12:40

No reliable Hebrew scholar would doubt that Jonah was in the belly of a whale for 3 full days and 3 full nights (72 hours). Jesus Christ stated that He would also ***be in the heart of the earth***

for 3 days *and* 3 nights, or a consecutive period of time = (3*12) + (3*12) = *72* hours (Matthew 12:40, John 11:9). All biblical scholars agree that Christ was placed in the grave just before 6:00 PM on Nisan 14. Now, we should note that the time which Jonah spent in the belly of the whale did not start when he was cast overboard from the boat, but from when he was swallowed up by the great whale. There was a short period of time during which He was "in the water" and a full period of time that he spent in the belly of the great fish. He stayed alive just long enough to pray to God (Jonah 2:1). To fulfill type he then died and when he was finally brought up from the depths of the sea 3 days and 3 nights later, he became alive again. The type of Jonah and the antitype of Christ is unmistakable: (1) Both suffered and died before "giving up the ghost"(2) Both were *swallowed up in death* (3) Both prayed to the Father for strength before dying (4) Both were dead for a period of 3 days and 3 nights and then resurrected from the *depths* of the grave.

Why has there been such controversy and confusion over how long Jesus Christ lay in the tomb? He clearly said it would be 3 days and 3 nights. He never said anything such as: "Hey guys....do not get confused. I really did not mean to say that I would lay in the tomb for a full 3 days and 3 nights. To understand what I am telling you, check with a Jewish Rabbi and Jewish oral tradition". *Did Christ forget to tell His disciples and us the entire truth?*

We will shortly show beyond reasonable doubt that Christ was placed in the tomb just before 6:00 PM on Nisan 14 and He rose from the grave late Saturday, Nisan 17. The type of Jonah and the whale would not be fulfilled by the antitype unless Jesus Christ would lie in the tomb for 3 consecutive days and 3 consecutive nights, just as Jonah was in the belly of the great fish for 3 consecutive days and nights. Christ had to be placed in the sepulture before 6:00 PM because: (1) It was against the Law of Moses to leave anyone who had been crucified on the cross after dark (Deuteronomy 21: 22-23) and (2) It was against Jewish "law" to bury someone on the Sabbath or on Jewish holidays (Torah). This is why Jesus had to be sealed in the tomb before 6:00 PM, which started Nisan 15...a *High Sabbath* day. There is another Jewish religious belief which will explain why Jesus had to lie in the tomb for a full 3 days and a full 3 nights. An unusual belief among the Jews was that when a person dies, that person will not be declared legally dead until a full 3 days and 3 nights have elapsed. If someone appeared to be dead and suddenly recovered before 3 days and 3 nights have passed, then that person was declared to have never been dead. This explains an incident that happened during the second year of Christ' 3.5 year ministry. Christ had a close personal relationship with Lazarus and his daughter Mary who lived in the town of Bethany (John 11:1). Christ was not in Judea when He received word that His friend Lazarus was near death and asked to come immediately. He then did a strange thing: He did not immediately go to Lazarus, but waited two days (John 11:6).

[**11**] *...and after that he saith unto them, Our friend Lazarus sleeps; but I go, that I may awake him out of sleep*

[**12**] *Then said his disciples, Lord, if he sleep, he shall do well (be healed)*

[**13**] *Howbeit Jesus spoke of his death: but they thought that he had spoken of taking of rest in*

sleep.
[**14**] *Then said Jesus unto them plainly, Lazarus is dead*   John 11: 11-14

Then when Jesus came, he found that he had lain in the grave ***four days*** *already*   John 11:17

When Jesus reached Bethany, he had already been dead for more than 3 days and 3 nights. He prayed to the Father and thanked Him that He had heard His prayer, and Lazarus arose from the grave.

[**43**] *.....he cried with a loud voice, Lazarus, come forth.*
[**44**] *And he that was dead came forth*   John 11: 43-44

Lazarus was *dead* (John 11:14). When Jesus raised Lazarus from the dead He showed His disciples that just as Lazarus was raised from the dead, he would also conquer death. When Christ was crucified on Nisan 14, He believed that the same power and authority that raised Lazarus would raise Him from the dead (John 11:4). We have already presented evidence that Jesus Christ was crucified on Nisan 14 at 3:00 PM. He was carried to the tomb of Joseph of Arimathaea (John 19:38) and was placed in the tomb just before 6:00 PM, which began the *High Sabbath day* of Nisan 15. He would arise from the tomb after 3 days and 3 nights just as He said that He would. Assume for now that Christ said what He meant and meant what He said: *He would lie in the grave for a full 3 days and 3 nights.* There are two possible ways that this statement can be interpreted. The most natural interpretation is that Christ meant 3 *consecutive* 24 hour days (72 hours) starting at 6:00 PM on Nisan 14. The second interpretation is that Christ meant that He would lie in the grave for 36 hours of daylight and 36 hours of darkness, starting at the moment that Christ was placed in the grave just before 6:00 PM on Nisan 14. There is *no question* that Jesus was placed in the sepulture just before 6:00 PM on Nisan 14. For illustrative and discussion purposes, suppose that Jesus was placed in the tomb at 5:45 PM on Nisan 14. Consider the following graphic.

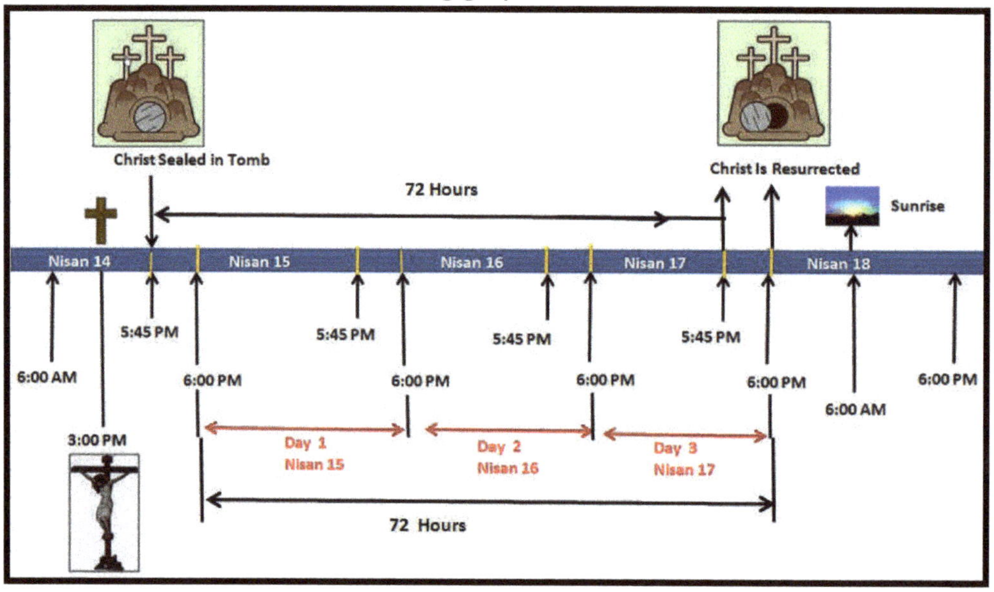

Jesus Christ said in Matthew 12:40 that He would lie in the grave for 3 days and 3 nights. The duration of 3 days and 3 nights is 72 consecutive hours: 36 hours of daylight and 36 hours of darkness. Note that Christ could possibly lie in the grave longer than 3 days and 3 nights....but no less. There are two cases to consider:

Case 1: The 72 hours are measured from when He was placed in the tomb at, say, 5:45 PM
Case 2: The 72 hours are measured from when night starts at 6:00 PM

There were several occasions when Christ spoke of His death, burial and resurrection.

- *From that time forth began Jesus to shew unto his disciples, how that he must go unto Jerusalem, and suffer many things of the elders and chief priests and scribes, and be killed, and* ***be raised again the third day*** Matthew 16:21

In Matthew 16:21, Christ reveals 3 things: (1) He must *suffer many things* (2) He will be slain (*killed*) and (3) He *would rise on the 3rd day*. The term *be raised* clearly implies that He rose from the tomb, and not from the cross. The 1st day is Thursday; the 2nd day is Friday; and the 3rd day is Saturday.

Case 1: Christ would rise between 5:45 PM on Nisan 16 and 5:45 PM on Nisan 17
Case 2: Christ would rise between 6:00 PM on Nisan 17 and 6:00 PM on Nisan 17

- The Son of man must suffer many things, and be rejected of the elders and chief priests and scribes, ***and be slain, and be raised the third day*** Luke 9:22
(Mark 9:31, 10: 33-34, Matthew 17:22, 20: 18-19)

Christ said that He would be *raised the 3rd day*. This is identical to Matthew 16:21,

- *Jesus answered and said unto them,* ***Destroy this temple****, and* ***in three days*** *I will raise it up* John 2:19

Christ said that after He was *destroyed* (killed) He would *rise in* (inside, within) *3 days*

Case 1: Christ would rise on either the 1st, 2nd or 3rd day after he had been killed, but no later than 5:45 PM on Nisan 17.
Case 2: Christ would rise on either the 1st, 2nd or 3rd day after he had been killed, but no later than 6:00 PM on Nisan 17.

- And he began to teach them, that the Son of man must suffer many things, and be rejected of the elders, and of the chief priests, and scribes, and ***be killed****, and* ***after three days*** *rise again* Mark 8:31 (Matthew 27:63)

Christ said that He would rise *after 3 days.*

Case I: He would rise after 5:45 PM on Saturday
Case 2: Christ would rise after 6:00 PM on Saturday

At first glance, Jesus seemed to contradict Himself, but the difficulties can be resolved if we carefully note what Christ said on 4 separate occasions. All prophecies can be resolved by recognizing that Matthew 12:40, Matthew 16:21, Mark 8:31, Luke 9:22 and John 2:19 are all simply stating three related facts: (1) Christ would be killed and Christ would be raised *on the 3rd day* (Matthew 16:21 and Luke 9:2). (2) Christ would be raised *in 3 days* (John 2:19) and that (3) Christ would be raised *after 3 days* (Mark 8:31). If Christ would be resurrected *no later* than at the end of 3 days and 3 nights or 72 hours (John 2:19)...and if he would not be resurrected until *after* 3 days and 3 nights or 72 hours (Matthew 27:63, Matthew 12:40) then there are only two possible times at which Jesus Christ was raised from the dead.

- *Just before 6:00 PM on Saturday, Nisan 17 in 30 AD* ***exactly*** 72 hours from when He was placed in the tomb on Wednesday, Nisan 14.

- At ***exactly*** 6:00 PM on Saturday, Nisan 17 after a consecutive period of 72 hours starting at 6:00 PM on Wednesday, Nisan 14

It is impossible to state with 100% confidence which is truth, but consecutive full periods of 3 nights (6:00 PM-6:00 AM) and 3 days (6:00 AM-6:00 PM) are indicated. This would place the resurrection at 6:00 PM on Saturday, Nisan 17. In fact, there is only *one moment in time* at which Christ would rise to exactly satisfy all scripture. Putting *everything* together, the truth is that **Christ must rise from the grave no later than exactly 6:00 PM on Saturday.** At exactly 6:00 PM Jesus Christ would have one foot in the tomb and one foot out of the tomb as He came forth. *Why would this conclusion be startling to anyone?* The same God who made the heavens and the earth; the same God that knows every hair on every head (Luke 12:7, Matthew 12:30); and the same God who raised Christ from the dead will raise all true believers in His only son at the last trumpet can without a doubt know when to exactly raise His only Son from the sepulture! That monumental event had been planned since the beginning of time.

The exact time that Christ rose from the grave was without a doubt either at 6:00 PM on Saturday or shortly before that time when His body was placed in the tomb. It is really not that important. What is important is that Jesus did rise from the grave and that He did so after 3 full days and 3 full nights in the grave at the end of Saturday, Nisan 17 .....and not on Sunday.

Since there can be no contradiction in the scriptures, look at what was said in Matthew 27 when the Jews came to Pontius Pilate and asked that the tomb be guarded.

Saying, Sir, we remember that that deceiver said, while he was yet alive, ***After three days*** *I will rise again* Matthew 27:63

It appears that the Roman Centurions understood that Christ would rise from the grave *after* 3 days. It is also certain that Pontius Pilate and the Jews were convinced that Christ would rise after 3 days and 3 nights starting on Nisan 14.

Command therefore that the sepulcher be made sure until the third day, lest his disciples come by night, and steal him away, and say unto the people, He is risen from the dead: so the last error shall be worse than the first Matthew 27:64

It has been shown that Christ was crucified was on Wednesday. Can we present any other convincing evidence that *Jesus Christ died on a Wednesday*?
No one doubts that Christ was crucified on Nisan 14, but there is widespread and heated disagreement among biblical scholars as whether Nisan 14 was a Wednesday, Thursday or Friday. It will now be shown conclusively that Wednesday, Nisan 14 was the day that Christ was crucified and that He arose from the grave just at the end of Saturday, Nisan 17. The following graphic shows the exact timetable if Christ was Crucified on a Wednesday.

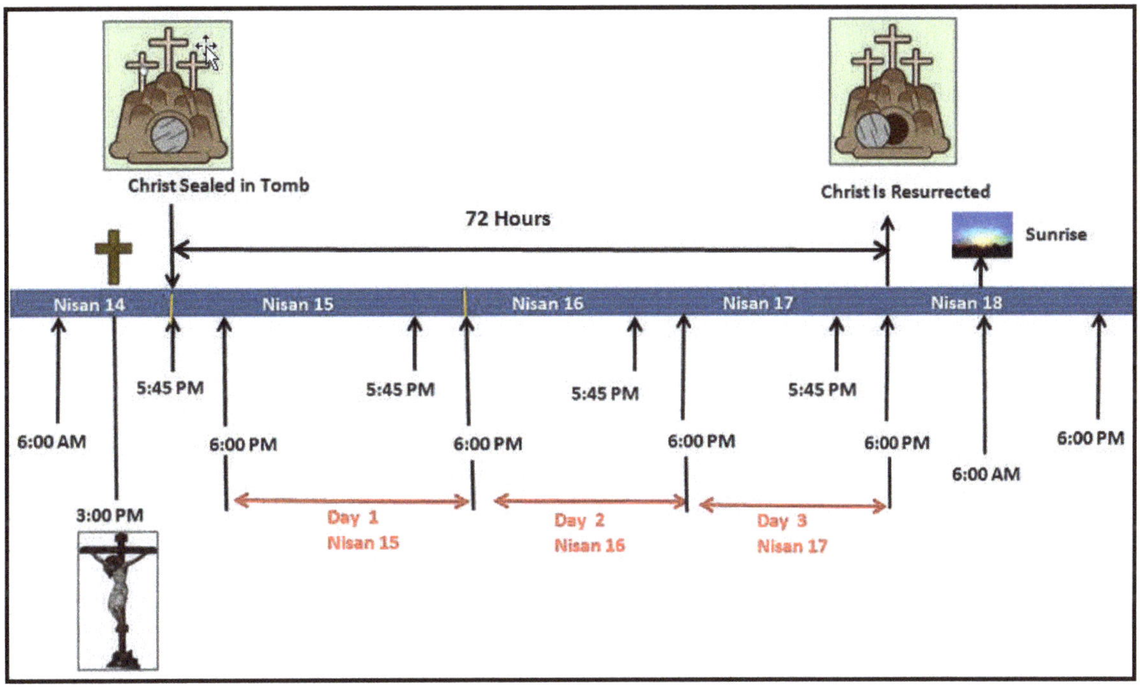

A Wednesday, Nisan 14 Crucifixion

If Christ was *in the grave* for a full 3 days and 3 nights, Nisan 14 was a Wednesday; Nisan 15 (1st day of Feast of Unleavened Bread) was a Thursday; Nisan 16 was a Friday; and Nisan 17 was a Saturday. Christ said that He would rise *after three days and 3* nights (Matthew 27:63).

There are two possibilities. Christ was placed in the tomb at: (1) 5:45 PM on *Wednesday, Nisan 14* and would rise immediately after 5:45 PM on *Saturday, Nisan 17* or Christ was referring to consecutive 3 days and 3 nights. In that case: (2) The 3 days and 3 nights would begin at 6:00 PM on Nisan 14 and ended immediately after 6:00 PM on Saturday, Nisan 17. The following table shows that Nisan 14 was on a Wednesday only in 30 AD between the years 29 AD - 33 AD. almost all chronologists and biblical scholars agree that Christ died between these four years.

Dates for the Jewish Passover (29 AD-33 AD)

Year	Jewish Calendar Date	Roman Calendar Date	Calendar Day
29 AD	Nisan 14	April 16	Saturday
30 AD	Nisan 14	April 5	Wednesday
31 AD	Nisan 14	March 26	Monday
32 AD	Nisan 14	April 14	Monday
33 AD	Nisan 14	April 3	Friday

A Friday, Nisan 14 Crucifixion

The following graphic shows the timeline of a Friday crucifixion.

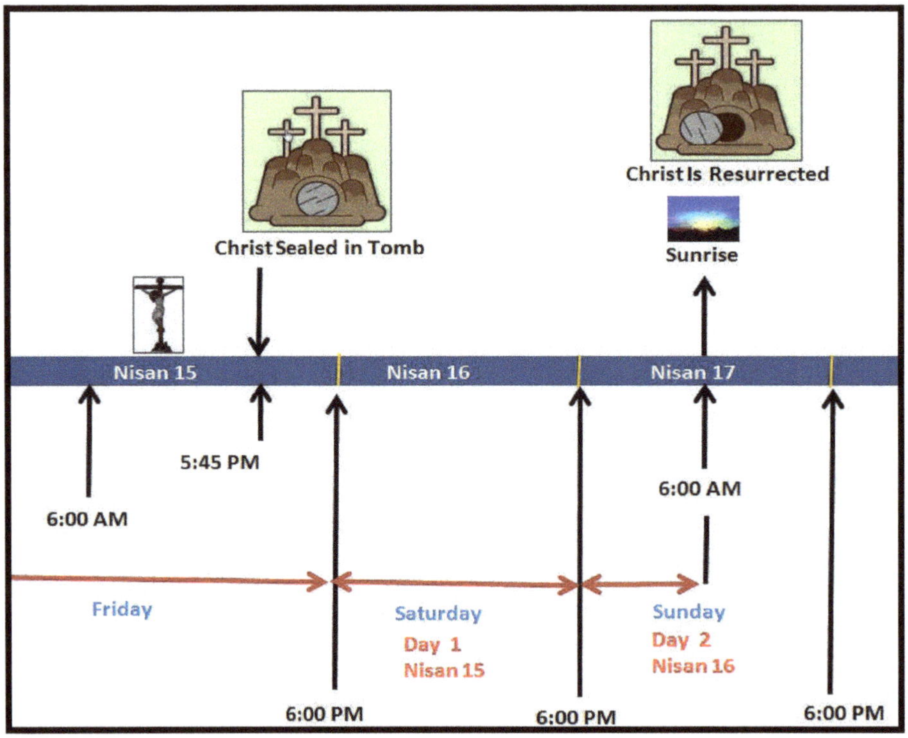

Millions of Christians and the Roman Catholic Church dogmatically and emphatically maintain that Christ was crucified on a Friday. Millions of Christians from many denominations celebrate the resurrection of Christ on Sunday morning at daybreak. This is known as *Easter* or *Resurrection Sunday*.

We have previously shown that Nisan 14 was a Friday only in 33 AD over the range of years that everyone believes Christ was crucified. This is one reason why anyone who equates Nisan 14 to a Friday believes that Christ was crucified in 33 AD. As it always does, the *Feast of Unleavened Bread* started on Nisan 15, which was a Saturday in 33 AD. Hence, Nisan 15 was *both* a High Sabbath Day and a weekly Sabbath day.....a "double Sabbath". Another reason that so many people hold dogmatically to a Friday, Nisan 16 resurrection comes from Mark.

And now when the even was come, because it was the preparation, that is, the day before the ***Sabbath*** Mark 15:42

Note that this is absolutely true, and when the Catholic Church institutionalized a Friday, Nisan 14 crucifixion and an early Sunday morning , Nisan 17 resurrection it was based upon the Sabbath of Mark 15:42 being the Jewish *weekly Sabbath of Saturday*. The fact that Nisan 15 was also a Sabbath day (High Sabbath day) was only a coincidence. Not only did the Roman catholic Church declare that Christ was crucified on Friday, Nisan 14 in 33 AD....... they also declared that Christ rose from the dead on Sunday morning just as day was breaking and the sun was coming up. At the First Council of Nicaea (325) the Roman Catholic Church decreed that Easter should be observed throughout the church to commemorate the resurrection of Christ. The date of Easter Sunday is not fixed each year, but it always falls on a Sunday between March 21 and April 25. Easter is always observed on the first Sunday after the monthly full moon, based on mathematical calculations.

The real problem is in trying to reconcile a Friday crucifixion and a Sunday morning resurrection with the words of Jesus is that Jesus said He would remain in the grave for 3 days and 3 nights and then rise. From the previous graphic we arrive at the following conclusions if Christ was crucified on a Friday and arose at the beak of day on Sunday, Nisan 16.

- Christ was placed in the tomb and the tomb was sealed shortly before 6:00 PM on Friday, Nisan 14. He was in the grave only a few minutes before the weekly Sabbath day on Saturday on Nisan 15.

- Christ lay in the grave for 1 full day on Saturday... 6:00 AM, Nisan 15 - 6:00 PM, Nisan 15.

- Christ would lie in the grave 1/2 day between 6:00 PM on Saturday, Nisan 16 - 6:00 AM, Sunday, Nisan 16

- Christ would rise at dawn on Sunday morning, Nisan 16

Clearly, the amount of time that Christ would lie in the grave would be 1.5 days or 36 hours plus a few minutes on Friday, Nisan 14 before 6:00 PM. At first glance, it seems that there is no way to claim that Christ spent 3 days and 3 nights in the grave. The solution to this problem can be found in the following statement.

> *A day in the bible is usually 24 hours long, but Jewish belief in the 1st century AD was that any part of a 24 hour day could be counted as a full day*

The scriptural support for this belief is found in the Old Testament. Consider the following.

For seven days *they camped opposite each other, and* ***on the seventh day*** *the battle was joined* I Kings 20:29

And he said to them, Return to me again ***in three days.*** *So Jeroboam and all the people came to Rehoboam* ***on the third day*** *as the king had directed* II Chronicles 10: 5, 12

On the third day *Esther put on her royal robes and stood in the inner court of the palace, in front of the king's hall* Esther 5:1

To be able to say that Christ spent 3 full days and 3 full nights in the grave, we must assume that the very short time that Christ spent in the tomb of Joseph..... just before Friday, Nisan 14 was changing into Saturday, Nisan 15...... would be counted as an *entire 24 hour day.* Counting those few minutes late Friday afternoon before 6:00 PM as *one full day and one full night* we arrive at a total of 3 nights (Friday, Saturday and Sunday), and 2 days (Friday and Saturday) or 52 hours in the tomb. We are still short 12 hours. Here we are forced to again apply the principle that any portion of one Hebrew day can be counted as a full day. The Roman Catholic church and those who hold to a Friday crucifixion also believe that Christ rose at daybreak on Sunday, Nisan 16. Since Christ rose from the grave after spending the night of Sunday, Nisan 16 in the sepulture, these 12 hours of Sunday, Nisan 16 can be counted as a full day. We now have 3 full days and 3 full nights or 72 hours in the tomb..... magic ! This is *actually* (1) several minutes before 6:00 PM on Friday, Nisan 14 (2) one full night (Night of Saturday, Nisan 15) (3) one full 12 hours of daylight on Saturday, Nisan 15 and (4) one full night on Sunday, Nisan 16..... a period of time equal to only 1.5 days and a few minutes.

Sunday morning has been institutionalized as *Easter Sunday* or *Resurrection Sunday* by all modern Christian denominations. This is also based upon a violation of the Holy scriptures. Recall that Mary Magdalene came to the tomb alone as soon as she could. The apostle John wrote;

The first day of the week cometh Mary Magdalene ***early, when it was yet dark****, unto the sepulcher, and seeth the stone taken away from the sepulcher* John 20:1

If the bible is inerrant in its basic message and John is recording the truth, Mary Magdalene came to the tomb *while it was yet dark* and the tomb was already open and empty. Jesus Christ had already risen and it was not yet daylight. John 20:1 is a fatal blow to the Easter morning

Sunday services which celebrate the resurrection of Christ as the sun was rising. In the above scenario, this would e the morning of Sunday, Nisan 16. Should Christians even celebrate the resurrection of Christ as the sun rose on Sunday, Nisan 16 ?.....**Of course!** When Jesus was actually resurrected and rose from the grave is not nearly as important as the fact that He *did arise* from the grave and conquered death. However, this does not imply that as a Christian and a disciple of Jesus Christ the truth should be ignored.

ye shall know the ***truth****, and the* ***truth*** *shall make you free* John 8:32

Search the scriptures; for in them ye think ye have eternal life: and they are they which testify of me John 5:39

In the Old testament, there are many prophecies concerning the fact that Jesus Christ would suffer, scourged and scorned. There was a prophecy by King David that spoke of His resurrection.

[**8**] *I have set the LORD always before me: because he is at my right hand, I shall not be moved.*
[**9**] *Therefore my heart is glad, and my glory rejoices: my flesh also shall rest in hope.*
[**10**] *For thou wilt not leave my soul in hell; neither wilt thou suffer thine Holy One to see corruption* Psalms 16: 8-10

Peter explains to us that King David was speaking of Jesus Christ and His future resurrection.

[**29**] *Men and brethren, let me freely speak unto you of the patriarch David, that he is both dead and buried, and his sepulcher is with us unto this day.*
[**30**] *Therefore being a prophet, and knowing that God had sworn with an oath to him, that of the fruit of his loins, according to the flesh, he would raise up Christ to sit on his throne;*
[**31**] *He seeing this before spoke of the resurrection of Christ, that his soul was not left in hell, neither his flesh did see corruption.* Acts 2: 29-31

However, there is not a single prophecy in the Old Testament that addresses *how long* that Christ would lie in the grave until He was resurrected. This was not revealed until Christ spoke to the Saducees and Pharisees when they demanded a ***sign*** that He was the Son of God. Christ banked the validity of His entire 3.5 year by Christ in the New Testament and that He was the Son of God on only one *sign*, and that was the Sign of Jonah.........He would be in the heart of the earth for 3 days and 3 nights.

To doubt that Christ was in the sepulture for any less than 3 days and nights implies that Christ did not know what He was talking about when He referred to Jonah and the great fish as a prophetic example of His own burial and resurrection. As a part of the eternal Godhead, He was well aware of what happened to Jonah...He was there. If He really meant anything less than a full 72 hours then He would have told us (and the Apostles) so. For completeness, a Thursday crucifixion will also be discussed.

A Thursday Crucifixion

It is likely that few would even consider proposing a Thursday resurrection if not for the publication of a book called *The Coming Prince* by Sir Robert Anderson around the turn of the 20th century. Anderson conducted an investigation of when Christ was crucified, and proposed that Thursday, April 6 in 32 AD was the year and day of the crucifixion.

> *Sir Robert Anderson used lunar data to fix the date of the first day of the first month of the twentieth year of Artaxerxes (the day implied in Nehemiah) to March 14, 445 BC. He showed that, based on various apparent refererences to the Great Tribulation both as three and a half years and also as 1260 days, 360 days could be fixed as the length of what he called a "prophetic year". He fixed the end date to Sunday, April 6... 32 AD, which he offered as the date of the Triumphal Entry.* Anderson concluded that Christ was crucified on Thursday, Nisan 10 in 32 AD.
> https://ichthus77.com/2008/01/03/sir-robert-andersons-calculations-linking-daniels-seventy-weeks-prophecy-and-jesus-crucifixion/

Sun	Mon	Tue	W	Thu	Fri	Sat
Nisan 3792						
		1	2	3	4	5
6	7	8	9	10	11	12
13	14	15	16	17	18	19
20	21	22	23	24	25	26
27	28	29	30			

The Jewish and RomanCalendars in 30 AD

Sun	Mon	Tue	W	Thu	Fri	Sat
April 0032 AD						
		1	2	3	4	5
6	7	8	9	10	11	12
13	14	15	16	17	18	19
20	21	22	23	24	25	26
27	28	29	30			

The following observations were taken from Anderson's theory.

Anderson was sure that the 490 year prophecy of Denial 9:27 held the key to predicting when Christ was crucified. This is undoubtedly true, but Daniel's prophecy is very difficult to interpret and use. The prophecy of Daniel is an important topic of study, and it could in theory be used to predict when Jesus would be crucified. Using sophisticated mathematical analysis. Anderson arrived at a (prophesied) date for the crucifixion of Christ which was Thursday, April 10, 32 AD. His work has been widely accepted as correct for over 100 years. His investigation is to be respected and commended, but several of his assumptions have been severely challenged and criticized. Scholarly investigation has found that He incorporated several fatal errors in His work (See Bob Pickle for a complete analysis of how Anderson reached this conclusion....published in his book: *The Coming Prince* (http://www.pickle-publishing.com/papers/sir-robert-anderson.htm)

No one except those few who ascribe to Anderson's theory suggest Thursday, 32 AD as a possible date for the death of Christ. *It is simply impossible to reconcile this conclusion with the gospel accounts of the death of Christ*, particularly Matthew 12:40. It is not the purpose of this book to challenge and analyze his conclusions. The only thing that is of importance is that because of His work many people believe that Christ was crucified on a Thursday and that He rose from the grave on Sunday morning. The following diagram graphically shows the implications of a Thursday crucifixion and a Sunday morning resurrection.

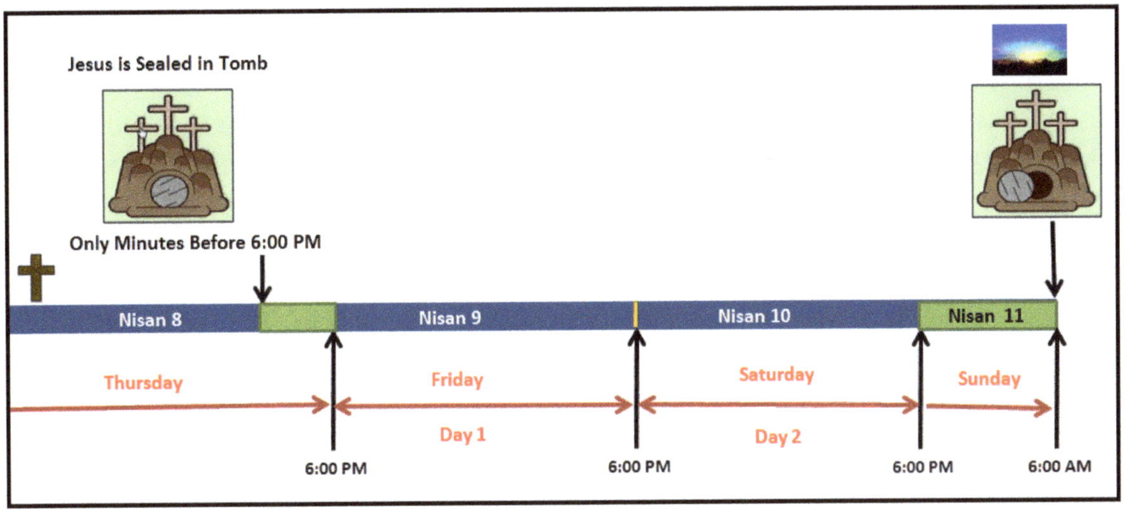

A Thursday crucifixion would result in: (1) Jesus being in the grave only a short time on Thursday, Nisan 8. (2) Christ would lay in the grave for two full days and two full nights on Friday, Nisan 9 and Saturday, Nisan 10. (3) Christ would spend 12 hours in the tomb Sunday night, Nisan 11. The total time that Christ would lay in the tomb is 2.5 days plus a few minutes on Nisan 8. This analysis shows that a Thursday crucifixion suffers from the same problems that does a Friday crucifixion: (1) The total time that Jesus Christ spent in the grave is not 3 full days and 3 full nights (2) The resurrection of Christ could not have occurred as the sun rose on Sunday, Nisan 11 (John 20:1). These problems can be solved by again invoking the (questionable) rule that *any portion of a day could count as a full day*. Hence, once again the short amount of time that Jesus spent in the grave on Thursday, Nisan 8 could be used to count the period of time between 6:00 AM and 6:00 PM. **But wait.....** If any portion of a day can count as a full day, then all day Thursday, Nisan 8 should be counted, and also all day Sunday, Nisan 11! This would yield 4 days and 4 nights in the tomb, which cannot be scripturally supported at all. Friends, you cannot have it both ways. Either way disqualifies a full period of 3 days and 3 nights in the sepulture.

Summary and Conclusions

The date, day and year that Jesus Christ the Son of God suffered and died on the Cross of Calvary has been a topic of intense inquiry for over 1900 years. It is believed that this Mystery has now been solved. A great deal of evidence has been presented to propose that Christ died on Wednesday, Nisan 14 in 30 AD and ***not*** on Friday, Nisan14 in 33 AD or on Thursday, Nisan 14 in 32 AD. . The death of Christ was on April 5 on the *Julian Calendar* that was in existence at that time.

The following events are believed to have happened in 30 AD.

- Jesus Christ was betrayed by Judas Iscariot in the Garden of Gethsemane on the Mt. of Olives around Midnight...... Wednesday night, Nisan 14.
- Christ is taken before Annus to be questioned shortly after midnight
- Christ is taken before Pilate and several members of the Sanhedrin during the night hours of Nisan 14 to build a case against Jesus.
- It is now late into the night of Nisan 14. Pilate retires to his house to get some rest, and Jesus is bound and escorted to spend the rest of the night in a cave beneath Herod's palace
- Jesus Christ is scourged, persecuted and beaten in a cave underneath the temple for the rest of the night
- Christ is put to trial before the Sanhedrin, the highest judicial court in all of Israel, shortly after daybreak on Nisan 14.
- Pilate finds out that Christ is from Nazareth...within the jurisdiction of Herod
- Christ is sent bound and sent to Herod for sentencing. Herod is in the temple for Passover.
- Herod can find no fault in Jesus, and returns Him back to Pilate
- Pilate can find no fault in Jesus, but an angry crowd seeks to put Jesus to death
- The crowd demands that Barabbas be released and that Christ is crucified in his Place
- Pilate frees a condemned criminal called Barabbas who has been sentenced to die by crucifixion, and condemns Jesus Christ to take his place
- Roman soldiers and the angry Jews lead Jesus off to be executed at a place called Golgotha on the Mt. of Olives
- Jesus is nailed to the cross at 9:00 AM on Wednesday morning
- Darkness falls over the entire land between 12:00 noon and 3:00 PM
- Jesus Christ "gives up the ghost" (dies) at 3:00 PM on Wednesday, Nisan 14
- When Christ dies there is a "great earthquake" and the veil in Herod's Temple which separates the Holy Place from the Holy of Holies is rent in two from top to bottom....The Glory and presence of God has departed
- A man named Joseph of Arithamaea requests that Pontius Pilate release the dead body of Jesus to him for burial
- Pilate grants the request of Joseph, and the body of Jesus is carried to the tomb which is near the crucifixion site
- The body of Jesus is hastily partially prepared for burial with precious oils and spices and wrapped in fine linen
- Christ is placed into the tomb just before 6:00 PM on Wednesday, Nisan 14. A large stone is placed at the sepulture entrance to prevent anyone from coming inside

- Thursday morning, Nisan 15 Pilate sends Roman soldiers to guard the tomb "until the third day"
- Jesus Christ lies dead in the tomb for a full period of 3 nights and 3 days
- Jesus Christ the Son of God is resurrected either just before 6:00 PM on Saturday, Nisan 17 or at exactly 6:00 PM on Saturday, Nisan 17.

This section has presented convincing evidence that Jesus Christ the Son of God was crucified on Wednesday, Nisan 14 in 30 AD and that He rose from the grave after a full 3 days and 3 nights at exactly 6:00 PM on Saturday, Nisan 17. A fact of equal importance to discovering the truth is that a Sunday morning resurrection just after daybreak at 6:00 PM is impossible.

The following observations are directly quoted from Fred R. Coulter in his book: *The Day That Jesus Christ Died.*

> ***When all of Jesus statements are taken into consideration, there is only one moment in time to which all can apply. At the end of the 3rd day on Saturday, Nisan 17 in 30 AD Jesus was resurrected.***

It has been shown that the death of Jesus Christ was on Wednesday, Nisan 14, in 30 AD on April 5 (Julian calendar date) and was resurrected on Saturday, Nisan 17 on April 8 in perfect harmony with all scriptural records as presented in the gospels of Matthew, Mark, Luke and John. Everything that happened between the death and resurrection of Jesus Christ is verified and supported by verse and scripture. *There is not a single contradiction of scripture.*

The exact time that Jesus Christ was resurrected cannot be stated with 100% confidence, but the time of resurrection has been narrowed down between minutes before 6:00 PM and 6:00 PM on Saturday, Nisan 17. This is a very narrow range of time, but this is not the most important conclusion of this study. The most important thing that can be stated with certainty is that Christ would rise before Sunday, Nisan 18 began.

Following the resurrection of Christ, there were visits to the tomb of Joseph by several women. There has been widespread confusion and Biblical interpretation of Matthew, Mark Luke and John concerning when the women visited the tomb after Christ had risen from the dead. We will show in the next chapter that when the correct chronology of all visits is properly determined and synchronized, there is really no confusion at all. In addition, the correct sequence of each visit will also fully support a Wednesday crucifixion and a late Saturday afternoon resurrection.

Daniels 70th Week and Christ Ministry

We have proposed and presented reasonable arguments to support a Nisan 14 (Wednesday, April 6) 30 AD crucifixion date for Jesus Christ. For more complete evidence that this is true, see Phillips and Coulter. The year 30 AD falls in the middle of Daniel's 70th week after 486.5 years have elapsed since the 490 year prophecy started. Clearly, this leaves 3.5 years to finish the prophecy. Many modern prophecy teachers allow the 70-7's to expire on Tishri 1 (Sept/Oct) of 33 AD. The event designated to end the prophecy is often proposed to be the stoning of Stephen in Acts 6. Proponents of this theory (rightly so) identify this event as the final act of rejection of Jesus Christ as the promised Messiah by the Corporate Nation of Israel. From this point on, the message of salvation in Jesus Christ under the New Covenant passed to the Gentiles. We totally reject the logic which ends Daniel's 70th week in 33 AD based upon two platforms: ***First***, we have already discussed in some detail the things which must be completed before Daniel's 70 weeks of years expires, and several things can only be accomplished at the second advent of Jesus Christ. This is reason enough to reject the ***Steven hypothesis***. A ***second*** and more compelling reason is in the stoning of Steven. In Acts 1-2 we are told how the Holy Spirit fell on the feast of Pentecost, 50 days after the resurrection. Chapter 3 records a post-Pentecost miracle, the healing of a lame man, followed by Peter's sermon. Chapters 4:1-6:7 are concerned with the beginning of persecutions and the preparation for spreading the gospel. Acts 6: 8 records how Steven ***full of faith and power*** did ***great wonders and miracles***. The Jewish leaders turned against him, fearing that he would ***destroy this place, and change the***

customs. At this point Stephen delivered perhaps the most powerful sermon ever preached (Acts 7: 1-53) . When he finished his discourse, the Jews cast him out of the city and stoned him. So, Steven became the first Christian to be martyred after the day of Pentecost. Now the conclusion: The conversion of Paul (Saul) is recorded in Acts 9. However, we know that this was within a year after Christ was crucified. Saul had witnessed the crucifixion of Christ, and then received a letter from Rome to further persecute and kill any Jew who would follow after Christ. It is impossible that the stoning of Steven took place 3.5 years after the crucifixion. We therefore conclude that there has been a "***gap***" of almost 2000 years since the midpoint of Daniel's 70th week. The *termination* of Daniel's 70th week will not occur until the second coming of Jesus Christ at the end of the great tribulation period. The ***third*** and most important reason is that when Christ was crucified on Passover, Nisan 14 in 30 AD He cried out that ***It is finished***. The agony, torture and persecution on the Cross of Calvary was finished......The sin issue was finished....and the Old Covenant was finished. Less than 24 hours earlier at the Lord's Last Supper, He arose and passed a Cup of Wine around to all of His apostles. He clearly said:

This is my blood of the new testament, which is shed for many for the remission of sins Matthew 26:28

In the original Greek language this should read:

28	τοῦτο	γάρ	ἐστιν	τὸ	αἷμά	μου	,	τῆς	διαθήκης	,	τὸ	περὶ	πολλῶν
	This	for	is	the	blood	of Me		of the	covenant		-	for	many

ἐκχυννόμενον	εἰς	ἄφεσιν	ἁμαρτιῶν	.
being poured out	for	forgiveness	of sins	

When Jesus Christ died on the Cross of Calvary He died for the forgiveness of all sins, and his sacrificial death initiated (by His own words) the ***New Covenant***. The Dispensation of the Law and the Old Covenant was finished and the New Covenant had begun. Note that up until this point in time that Jesus had gone to the Jews first, but now He would turn to the Gentiles. This and the Age of Grace was completely hidden and unknown to the Jews....It was a mystery revealed by the Apostle Paul. Salvation would now be by faith and grace, to both Jew and Gentile alike. Please do not miss the implication of this truth. God had been dealing with the Jews ever since the Daniel prophecy began in 458 BC. He continued to deal with the Jews...not the Gentiles...until Christ was crucified on the Cross of Calvary. Daniel is a Jewish prophecy, and when God turned away from them and offered salvation to the Gentiles it would be interrupted before it would be completely fulfilled. The entire church age was a *gap in time* which was not known before Paul revealed its mystery. *When will God once more begin dealing with the* *corporate Jews*? All prophecy scholars agree that the 70th week of Daniel will be resumed when the Great Tribulation begins.

We have already thoroughly discussed the things that were to be accomplished by the end of Daniel's 70th week, and all of those things will not be fully accomplished until the end of the *Age of Grace*, or the *Church Age*. Daniels last week (7 years) of the 70 week prophecy is not interrupted with 7 years remaining when He came to be baptized by John, but it would continue for another 3.5 years as Christ preached to the Jews...not to the Gentiles.

These twelve Jesus sent forth, and commanded them, saying, ***Go not into the way of the Gentiles****, and into any city of the Samaritans* ***enter ye n****ot* Matthew 10:12

Why has this been so hard to believe? The earthly ministry of Christ as recorded in Matthew, Mark, Luke and John was to the JEWS....not the Gentiles. Once understood, it is inconceivable that these 3.5 years would not be contiguously contained within the initial part of Daniels 70 week prophecy to the Jews. *Does this fit with the duration of the Great Tribulation?* Not only does it fit, but it makes perfect sense. The Wrath of Satan and the Wrath of God does not take place until after Satan is cast down to earth in Revelation 12. The Antichrist will not arise until Revelation 13. Satan is allowed to persecute all Jews and Gentiles for approximately 3.5 years.

It has always intrigued this author that the earthly ministry of Jesus Christ lasted 3.5 years and that the period of time that Satan will attack and kill as many Christians as he can in the Great Tribulation is also 3.5 years in duration. This now makes perfect sense once it is realized that the 70 week prophecy of Daniel is dealing with a prophecy to the Jews, and no one else. The earthly ministry of Christ will begin 483 years after Nebuchadnezzar issued a decree to Ezra the scribe which began the 490 year prophecy. Christ will be dealing with the Jews for another 3.5 years until He is crucified. There will then be a "gap in time" as God turns to the Gentiles and the Church Age takes place. The last 3.5 years of Daniels prophecy will resume once again when Satan begins His 3.5 year reign of terror against all Jews and Christians. Until these last 3.5 years of the Daniel prophecy begin, there will be tribulation as prophesied by Christ in Matthew 24. Christ Himself said that we are to be aware that this persecution is **not the end.**

[**7**] *For nation shall rise against nation, and kingdom against kingdom: and there shall be famines, and pestilences, and earthquakes, in divers places.*
[**8**] *All these are the beginning of sorrows* Matthew 24: 7-8

Study to shew thyself approved unto God, a workman that need not to be ashamed, ***rightly*** *dividing the word of truth* II Timothy 2:16

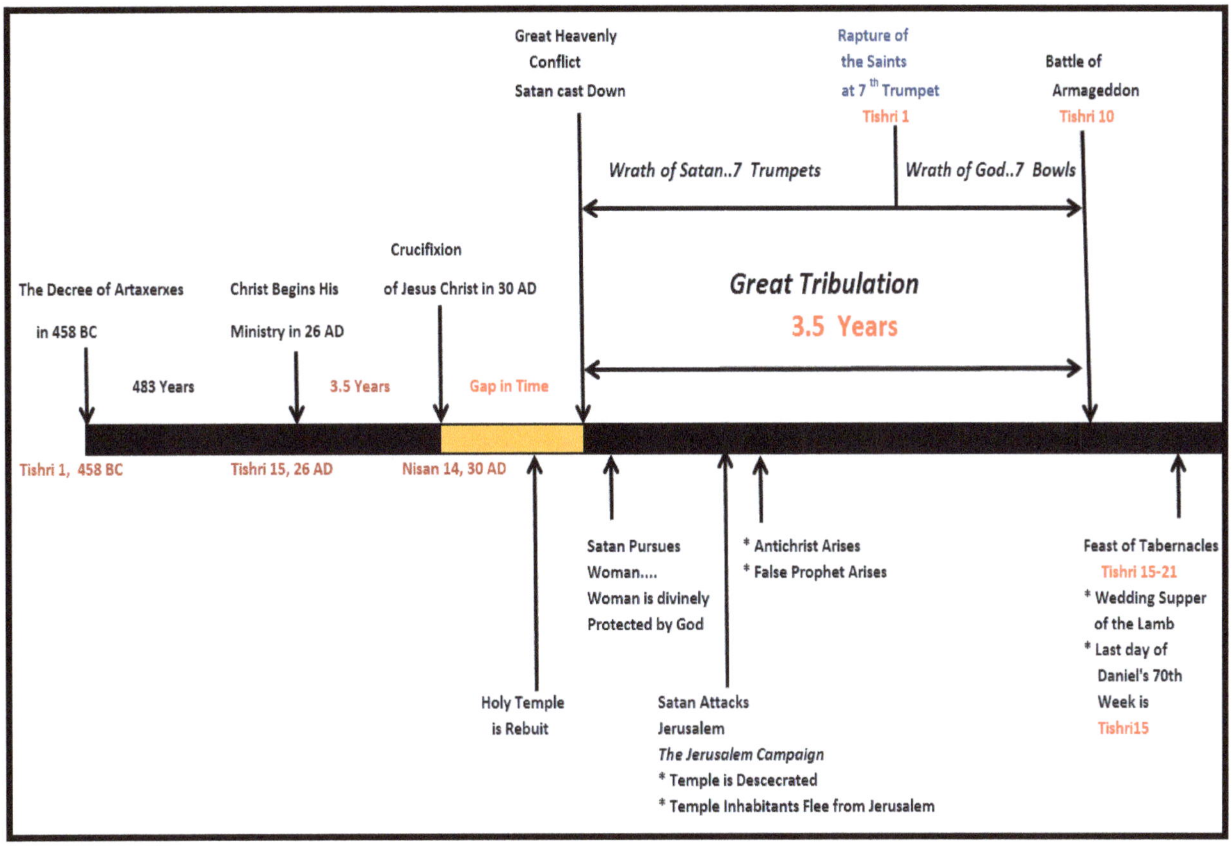
Great Heavenly
Conflict
Satan cast Down
Rapture of
the Saints
at 7 th Trumpet
Tishri 1
Battle of
Armageddon
Tishri 10
Wrath of Satan..7 Trumpets
Wrath of God..7 Bowls
Crucifixion
of Jesus Christ in 30 AD
The Decree of Artaxerxes
in 458 BC
Christ Begins His
Ministry in 26 AD
Great Tribulation
3.5 Years
483 Years
3.5 Years
Gap in Time
Tishri 1, 458 BC
Tishri 15, 26 AD
Nisan 14, 30 AD
Satan Pursues
Woman....
Woman is divinely
Protected by God
* Antichrist Arises
* False Prophet Arises
Feast of Tabernacles
Tishri 15-21
* Wedding Supper
of the Lamb
* Last day of
Daniel's 70th
Week is
Tishri15
Holy Temple
is Rebuit
Satan Attacks
Jerusalem
The Jerusalem Campaign
* Temple is Descecrated
* Temple Inhabitants Flee from Jerusalem

Chapter 5

Daniel and Jewish Destiny

The Book of Daniel is the most comprehensive source of prophecy in the entire body of scripture. Daniel was deported from Israel to the Babylonian Empire around 606 BC in the first wave of captives. He was a very young man and was taken to Babylon with Shadrach, Meshach and Abednego...all of which were still in their 'teens. About 20 years later, in 586 BC, the City of Jerusalem and the Temple were both destroyed by the Babylonian army and all but the old and feeble were taken in exile for a period of 70 years. This devastation and deportation was because Israel failed to pay tribute to the Babylonian Empire, but the real reason was an act of God for Israel failing to let the land rest every 7th year (Sabbatical year) for over 490 years. As the 70 years neared an end, Daniel realized from reading the Book of Ezekiel that the captivity was almost over and He asked God to show him the future of his brethren, the Jews. God responded to Daniel by showing him what would befall the Jews in future years. This is recorded in Chapters 7-11. Daniel may not have fully understood the scope of his prophecies, but in Daniel Chapter 9 the panorama of what would happen many years later was revealed, stretching from when a decree was issued by Artaxerxes in his 7th year of reign (458 BC - 457 BC) to restore the temple and rebuild the Holy City (49 years). The prophecy spanned a period of time from the departure of Ezra to the coming of a Messiah who would redeem Israel (483 years)....up to the death of Jesus Christ (486.5 years) ....to the last half of Daniel's 70th and last week when Christ would come again and finally restore Israel to a covenant relationship with God: And so *all of Israel will be saved*. Although the prophecies of Daniel were to give him *skill and understanding*, he was probably bewildered and confused. So a *man clothed in linen* (Daniel 10:5) was sent to show him the meaning of this prophecy. This was likely the Archangel Michael (Daniel 11:1). The conclusion of the matter is found in Daniel 12: 1-13. It seems proper that we should also understand this final revelation to Daniel.

*And **at that time** shall Michael stand up, the great prince which stands for the children of thy people: and there shall be a time of trouble, such as never was since there was a nation even to that same time: and at that time thy people shall be delivered, every one that shall be found written in the book* Daniel 12:1

Michael is a very powerful angel who is called an *archangel* in Jude 9. He is also called one of the *Chief Princes* in Daniel 10:13. When *Gabriel* was sent to Daniel in Daniel 10, Gabriel was detained for 21 days because Satan warred against him. It was Michael who came to help Gabriel and together they were finally able to overcome their celestial adversaries (Daniel 10:13). Michael will personally encounter Satan again on two other occasions: One is when

Michael will argue with Satan about whether Moses was buried or translated to heaven (Jude 9). The other is in Revelation 12 when Satan and his fallen angels will wage war in the heavenlies against Michael and his holy angels (Revelation 12: 1-11) . Michael is also called *the great protector of the Jews* (Daniel 12:1). *At that time* is just before the last half of Daniel's 70th week starts, which is also the last 3.5 years of the Church Age. Michael will arise with his holy angels and defeat Satan....casting him down to earth (Revelation 12: 7-8). Then there will be a time of trouble, *great trouble*.... which is the *Wrath of God* (Revelation 15:1, Revelation 16:1) and the *Wrath of Satan* (Revelation 12:12). These last 3.5 years are called the *time of Jacob's trouble* (Jeremiah 30:7). It will be such an intense time of persecution and tribulation that Jesus in His Olivet Discourse said:

[**21**] *For then shall be great tribulation, such as was not since the beginning of the world to this time, no, nor ever shall be.*
[**22**] *And **except those days should be shortened**, there should no flesh be saved: but for the elect's sake those days shall be shortened* Matthew 24: 21-22

The days which will be shortened will be the 1267 days of the last 3.5 years of Daniel's prophecy. The *days are shortened* when all believers are raptured out at the 7th trump on the Feast of trumpets, Tishri 1, and the shortened time will be the *ten days* between the *Feast of Trumpets* on Tishri 1 and the *Feast of Yom Kippur* on Tishri 10...a period of 10 days during which the *Wrath of God* is poured out upon the *desolate* (Daniel 9:27, Romans 1:18, I Thessalonians 5:9, Revelation 15:1, Revelation 11:18). At that time, corporate Israel will finally turn to Jesus Christ for their redemption. *All will be saved* who will accept Jesus Christ as their Lord and savior and will have their names inscribed in the *Book of Life* (Revelation 20:15).

[2] *And many of them that sleep in the dust of the earth shall awake, some to everlasting life, and some to shame and everlasting contempt*

[3] *And they that be wise shall shine as the brightness of the firmament; and they that turn many to righteousness as the stars forever and ever.* Daniel 12: 2-3

Daniel is assured that many will awake to eternal life....those Old Testament saints who died in the faith of Abraham that a Messiah would arise who would redeem them from sin. Until the time of redemption, a remnant of Jews who are called Messianic Jews will individually accept Christ as this church age continues to unfold, and there will be others that will turn to Jesus Christ and suffered death in the Great Tribulation, and even others who will die believing in Jesus Christ during the Millennial Kingdom. Sadly, many will die who refuse to believe that Jesus Christ is the Son of God and they will be cast into the Lake of Fire and Brimstone forever (Revelation 20: 12-15). Some refuse to believe this, but that is their choice.

They that were *wise* are all who believe in faith. Both the Old Testament Jews who died in faith and those today that work faithfully to save their brethren.... *they that turn many to righteousness*...will shine brightly as the stars that are in the heaven.

But thou, O Daniel, shut up the words, and seal the book, even to the time of the end: many shall run to and fro, and knowledge shall be increased Daniel 12:4

Daniel is told to *shut up* or finish recording the words and prophecies that he has been given. *Seal the book* means to record the words and do not add or detract from anything revealed. Many days and many people will come and go, and knowledge will be increased. At the end of WW II, knowledge was said to be doubling every 26 years. Today, it is doubling about every 13 months. The technology used in this book was not available 100 years ago, and computers now allow for instant knowledge access.

[5] *Then I Daniel looked, and, behold, there stood other two, the one on this side of the bank of the river, and the other on that side of the bank of the river.*
[6] *And one said to the man clothed in linen, which was upon the waters of the river, How long shall it be to the end of these wonders?* Daniel 12: 5-6

As Daniel is standing beside the *River Tigris*, he suddenly sees three angels. An angel is standing on each side of the River and one is standing upon the water. The two angels which stand on the banks seem to be curious about what all of this means, and they turn to the one angel standing upon the water and ask: *How long will it be until all of these prophecies come to pass?* The context of this question and its response are not how many years in the future will pass until all of these things are finished, but how long will it be after the Man of Sin or the Antichrist will arise until all of these things will come to an end.

And I heard the man clothed in linen, which was upon the waters of the river, when he held up his right hand and his left hand unto heaven, and swore by him that lives forever that it shall be for a time, times, and an half; and when he shall have accomplished to scatter the power of the holy people, all these things shall be finished Daniel 12:7

This is a confirmation that the period of extreme persecution and tribulation is not 7 years as many claim but only a time, times and half-a-time, or 3.5 years..... or 1267 days...... or the last half of Daniels 70th week.

Daniel hears the man...who is clothed in linen..... answer the other two angels: It will be for a *time, times and half-a-time*. This phrase has been encountered before in Daniel 7:25. It is a phrase which must be determined in context, and in Daniel 7:25 it refers to the time that Antiochus Epiphanies (will) desecrate the temple after the death of Alexander the Great. This was about 3.5 years until a brave band of people called the *Maccabees* recovered the Temple from the desecration of Antiochus. In Daniel 12:7 it refers to the end times when Antichrist will arise. This is the time that the *woman* (Revelation 12: 1, 14, 17) is persecuted by *Satan* (Revelation 12:9) as soon as she births the *Man-Child* (Revelation 12:5). This time has been shown to be 1267 days, which is the duration of the last 3.5 years of the Great Tribulation. When the *dispersion of the Jews shall be fully ended*, then the totality of these prophesied events shall be fulfilled. The restoration of the Jewish nation is foretold by all the prophets, and it is one of the key events which will come to pass in the latter days of this current age. The terminus quo of these 1267 days will be when Satan is defeated at the Battle of Armageddon, and the *dispersion of the Jews will be finished* when those who have finally turned to Jesus Christ as their prophesied Messiah, and survive the Great Tribulation will enter into the land promised to Abraham, Moses and King David long ago. These Jews will be real people... in real bodies... who will live on real, earthly land. They will live and die, procreate and farm the land. The Millennial Kingdom is completely described in Phillips, *The Millennial Kingdom: Life After the Great Tribulation*.

And I heard, but I understood not: then said I, O my Lord, what shall be the end of these things?
Daniel 12:8

Daniel heard what the angel in linen had said, but he was confused by the answer. He did not understand what it all meant, so he inquired again: *How long will it be until all of these prophecies come to pass?*

[9] *And he said, Go thy way, Daniel: for the words are closed up and sealed till the time of the end.*
[**10**] *Many shall be purified, and made white, and tried; but the wicked shall do wickedly: and none of the wicked shall understand; but the wise shall understand* Daniel 12: 9-10

The reply of the angel upon the waters could be viewed as somewhat condescending. He did not answer this question, but replied as follows: "Daniel, Gabriel has already told you many things and gave you wisdom and understanding. What do you mean you do not understand? Oh well...maybe that is to be expected, so just go your way. The words will be *closed up* until the *time of the end*. As the end nears, knowledge will be increased and much will be revealed to those who diligently inquire. As to your people: there are many who will be purified and cleansed of all sin, but these will be those who died in the faith of Abraham looking to a future redeemer. Those who are wise and trust in the Lord will *understand*, but those who are wicked and fail to believe will never understand".

[**5**] *Behold, the days come, saith the LORD, that I will raise unto David a righteous Branch, and a King shall reign and prosper, and shall execute judgment and justice in the earth.*
[**6**] *In his days Judah shall be saved, and Israel shall dwell safely: and this is his name whereby he shall be called, THE LORD OUR RIGHTEOUSNESS* Jeremiah 23: 5-6

And so ***all Israel shall be saved****: as it is written, There shall come out of Zion the Deliverer, and shall turn away ungodliness from Jacob* Romans 11:26

And from the time that the daily sacrifice shall be taken away, and the abomination that maketh desolate set up, there shall be a thousand two hundred and ninety days Daniel 12:11

This is perhaps the most difficult prophecy in scripture. In looking at many interpretations, none seem satisfactory . The starting point is known with certainty: *from the time that the daily sacrifice shall be taken away, and the abomination that maketh desolate set up*. This cannot refer to the sacrificial death of Christ as the Lamb of God when he ended temple sacrifice, because at that time an abomination that maketh desolate was not set up in the temple. This can only refer to when Satan and the Antichrist desecrates the temple and sets up an idol which will come to life and speak blasphemous things against God (Revelation 13:15). Those who will worship the Antichrist and Satan will be recognized by a mark of the Beast, which is *a mark in their right hand, or in their foreheads.* This is to identify those who worship Satan, and without this mark no one can buy or sell anything (Revelation 13:17). The notion that this mark is a computer chip under the skin is just pure speculation. It will be the name of the beast or the number of the beast....this is the number 666. In the Greek language, each letter of the alphabet also carries a specific number. The study of numeric's in the Holy Bible is called *Gematria*. It is quite easy to take a name and turn it into a number, but it is difficult to turn a number into a name. For example, the name Jesus in the Greek language is *Lesous* and its numerical value is 888. The number 8 is new order or new beginning, and three is completeness. It is a spiritually perfect number.

Greek Word for Jesus is *Iesous*					
Greek Numerical Equivalent					
I	**E**	**S**	**O**	**U**	**S**
10	8	200	70	400	200
Total = 888					

The number 6 means the *manifestation of sin*, 60 is the number of *personal pride* and 66 is the number of *idol worship*. Hence, the number 666 embodies pride, idol worship and is the name of the beast; or the number of his name.

The following diagram shows that there are 1260 days between when the temple is desecrated and the Battle of Armageddon (Revelation 11:3), on both a traditional timescale and the one proposed in Chapter 4.

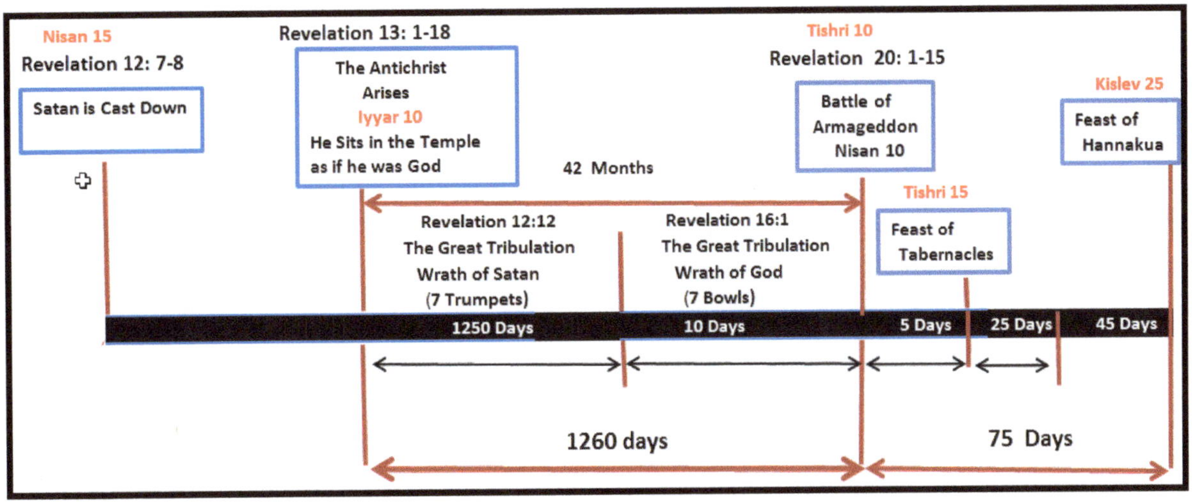

Daniel 12:11 reveals a period of 1260 days between when the Antichrist arises and the *Feast of Yom Kippur*, on which day the Battle of Armageddon will take place and the church age will come to an end. Counting off 30 more days beyond the Feast of Yom Kippur (Tishri 10) we arrive at *Heshvan 10*. This is an important day in Jewish history. It was on this day that Noah entered into the ark 1656 years after Adam and Eve were banned from the Garden of Eden (Phillips, *A Biblical Chronology from Adam to Christ*, 2nd Edition). It is not revealed to Daniel (or to us) what this date signifies, which is 30 days after the Great Tribulation comes to an end. We only know that it will be 30 days into the Millennial Kingdom. One of the most important things that will take place as the 1000 year Millennial Kingdom begins to unfold is that Christ will finally fulfill His covenant promise with Abraham, Moses and King David to restore the Promised Land to the children of Israel. The 144,000 Jews sealed in Revelation 7 and the *Sheep* in the Judgment of the Nations (Matthew 25: 31-46) will all inherit and live upon their own land for 1000 years. It will be a glorious time of peace and prosperity for the Jews. The land will yield its crops in abundance, every man will sit under his own fig tree and the animal kingdom will become as they were in the Garden of Eden before Adam and Eve fell from grace (Phillips,: The Millennial Kingdom; *Life After the Great Tribulation*). It can only be conjectured, but this day could be the day that the 12 tribes inherit the land. The angel clothed in linen now provides more information.

Blessed is he that waits, and cometh to the thousand three hundred and five and thirty days.
Daniel 12:12

To the average Christian, this is just another strange prophecy. It adds another 45 days to Nisan 10 for a total of 75 days. However, any Jew will recognize this date. It is Kislev 25, the 1st day of the *Feast of Hannakua* !!

Hanukkah is a significant day in the history of the Jews. In 174 BC a madman known as Antiochus III....who was also called Epiphanes.... began to reign over Syria. He invaded Israel and with superior forces he assaulted the temple in Jerusalem. After a short battle he gained control of the complex and the city. To the horror of all Jews, he slaughtered swine in the holy place and desecrated the temple. He blasphemed God and controlled the temple for over 3 years, at which time a rebel band of Jews led by a family called the *Maccabees* mounted a furious attack and drove off the Syrian soldiers. The Maccabees entered and cleansed the Temple, and then destroyed all of the idols placed there by the Syrian heathens. Judah Maccabees and his followers built a new altar, which he dedicated on Kislev 25 in 139 BC. Legend has it that a *Menorah* was constructed (A candle stick structure with 7 lights) to replace the one that had been stolen by the invaders. The original Menorah was constructed and placed in the Tabernacle of Moses. The lights were fueled by holy oil and in a search of the temple only a small cruse of oil was found....only enough for about one day. Legend also has it that by a divine act of God the small vessel of oil fueled the Menorah for 8 days. To commemorate this miracle, the Rabbis inaugurated the 8 day Feast of Hannakua starting on Kislev 25. It is a joyous occasion of thanksgiving and prayer, punctuated by the lighting of candles. Jesus spoke of this Feast during His ministry, and He said that: *I am the light of the world: he that followeth me shall not walk in darkness, but shall have the light of life* (John 8:12). It would be consistent with scripture and highly appropriate that on Kislev 25 the rebuilt temple complex in Jerusalem and the Millennial Throne of God would be dedicated. If this is true, there would be great celebration and feasting for 8 days. People will come from all over Israel to worship our Lord Jesus Christ. Is this the meaning of Daniel 12: 11-12 ? Only time will tell. A final question might be: *Will the ecclesia (those who are in Christ) be there?* The answer is, *Yes*. They will rule and reign with Christ for 1000 years and serve Him (Phillips; The Millennial Kingdom: *Life After the Great Tribulation*).

Blessed is he that waits, and cometh to the thousand three hundred and five and thirty days
Daniel 12:12

This seems to mean that anyone who has accepted Christ as their Lord and Savior and is still alive when The Feast of Hannakua is celebrated will be *blessed*. An appropriate translation could also be: *Those that wait for him* (Isaiah 64:4). Jesus repeatedly told those that will follow Him into eternity to *watch and wait*. Those that are still alive and remain will be blessed for sure...They will sit with our Lord Jesus Christ and lean on him in their mortal bodies. Of course, the resurrected dead in Christ in their glorious heavenly bodies will also be there.

But go thou thy way till the end be: for thou shalt rest, and stand in thy lot at the end of the days   Daniel 12:13

The angel concludes with such a blessing that it can only be described in glorious terms.

"Daniel, arise and go in peace. Just go about your normal daily business...continue to praise the Lord for what He will accomplish in your people and be not afraid". *You will rest*. This clearly has a double meaning. *You will rest* in peace throughout the remainder of your mortal life, then you will rest in paradise awaiting the Lord and the resurrection. In life or death you will know that He loves you and is watching over you: *You are greatly beloved* (Daniel 9:23). He then says the words that every Christian is longing to hear and clings to as we serve Him: "You will stand in thy lot at the end of the days. Oh Daniel, you will experience physical death but you will not die. The great Jewish redeemer yet to come will raise you from the grave and you will stand before Him in glory and honor".

And so will you if you accept Jesus Christ as your Lord and Savior. Are you secure in Christ?

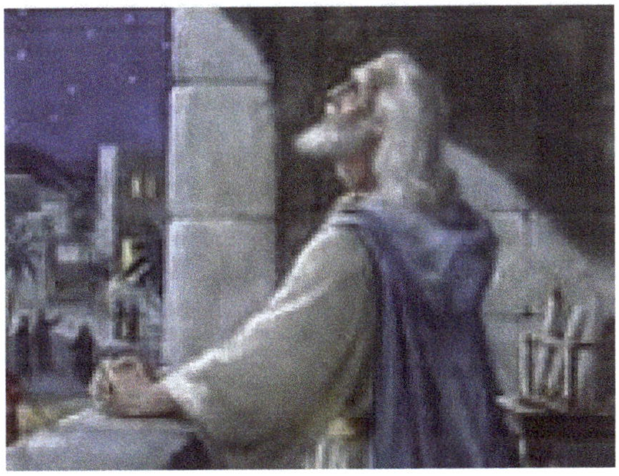

Bibliography

Phillips, Don T., The Book of Revelation: *Mysteries Revealed*, 2nd Edition, Virtual Bookworm. com, PO Box 9949, College Station, Texas 7784.

Phillips, Don T., The Book of Ruth: *Historical and Prophetic Truths* , Virtual Bookworm. com, PO Box 9949, College Station, Texas 7784.

Phillips, Don T., Life After Death: *Mysteries Revealed,* Virtual Bookworm. com, PO Box 9949, College Station, Texas 7784.

Phillips, Don T., The Eternal Plan of God: *Dispensations, Covenant Promises, Salvation,* Virtual Bookworm. com, PO Box 9949, College Station, Texas 7784.

Phillips, Don T., The Birth and Death of Christ, Virtual Bookworm. com, PO Box 9949, College Station, Texas 7784.

Phillips, Don T., The Book of Exodus: *Historical and Prophetic Truths* Virtual Bookworm. com, PO Box 9949, College Station, Texas 7784.

Phillips, Don T., A Biblical Chronology From Adam to Christ, Virtual Bookworm. com, PO Box 9949, College Station, Texas 7784.

Phillips, Don T., Life After the Great Tribulation: *The Millennial Kingdom* Virtual Bookworm. com, PO Box 9949, College Station, Texas 7784.

Phillips, Don T., The Last 50 Days of Jesus Christ Virtual Bookworm. com, PO Box 9949, College Station, Texas 7784.

Finegan, Jack, Handbook of Biblical Chronology, Hendrickson Publishing Company, Peabody, Ma.

Larkin, Clarence, Dispensational Truth, P.O. Box 334, Glenside, Pa., 1920

Logos apostolic Church of God and Bible College, Interlinear Greek and Hebrew Translation, Logos apostolic.org, United Kingdom, Logos apostolic.org

Ryrie, Charles C., The Ryrie Study Bible, King James Version, Moody Press, Chicago

Dake, Finis J., Dake's Annotated Reference Bible, Dake Bible Sales, P.O. Box 1050, Lawrenceville, Ga., 30246

Coulter, Fred R, The Day Jesus the Christ Died, York Publishing Company, PO Box 1038, Hollister, California

Coulter, Fred R, The Appointed Times of Jesus The Messiah, York Publishing Company, PO Box 1038, Hollister, California

Horn, S. H. and L.H. Wood, The Chronology of Ezra 7, TEACH Services, Inc., www.teachservices.com

Books by Don T. Phillips, www.phillips-bible-study-books.com

www.ingramcontent.com/pod-product-compliance
Lightning Source LLC
Chambersburg PA
CBHW060946100426
42813CB00016B/2878
* 9 7 8 1 9 5 1 9 8 5 6 9 1 *